GIRLS ON TOP 2

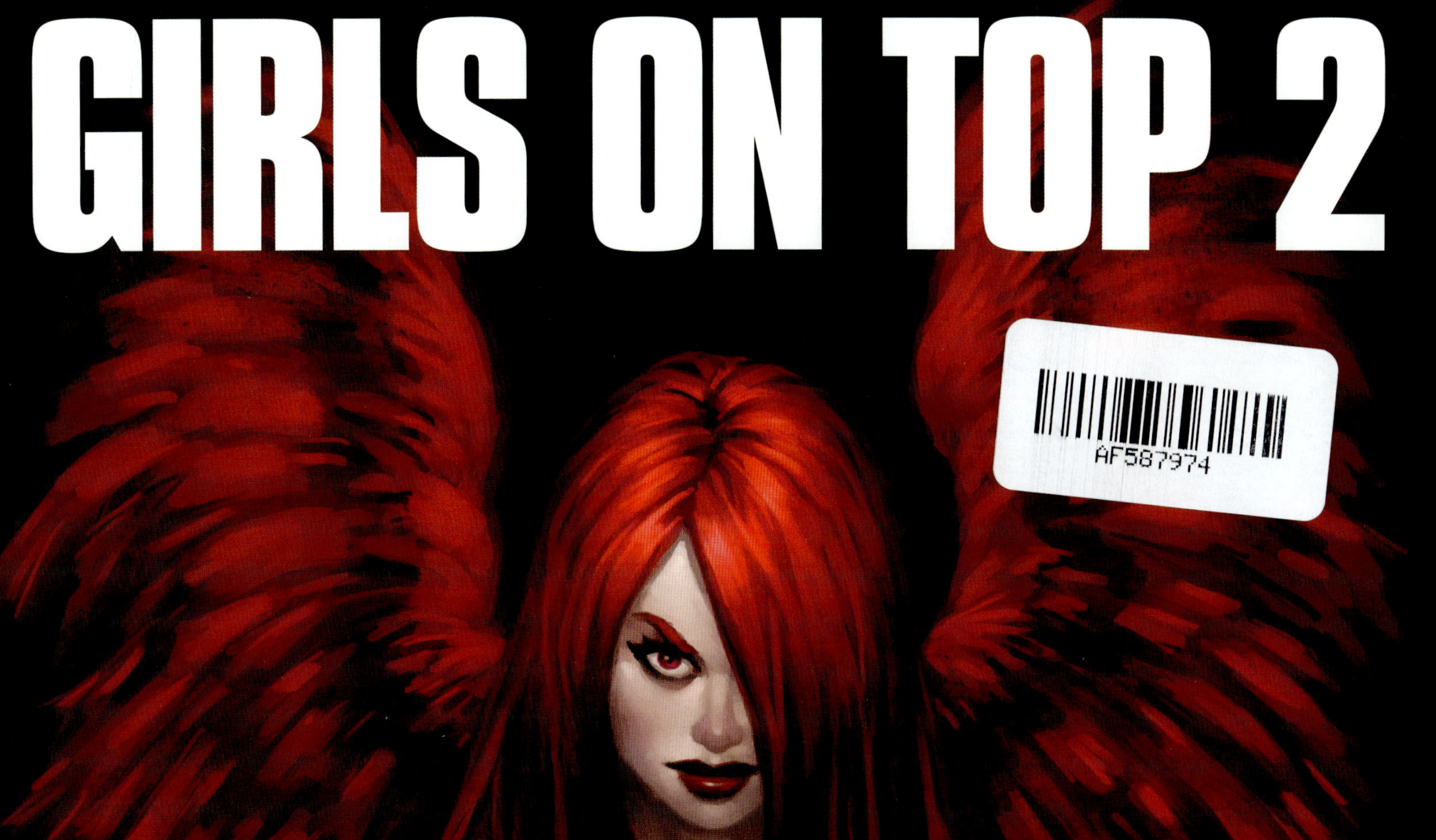

more pin-up art of Matt Dixon

AN SQP PRESENTATION

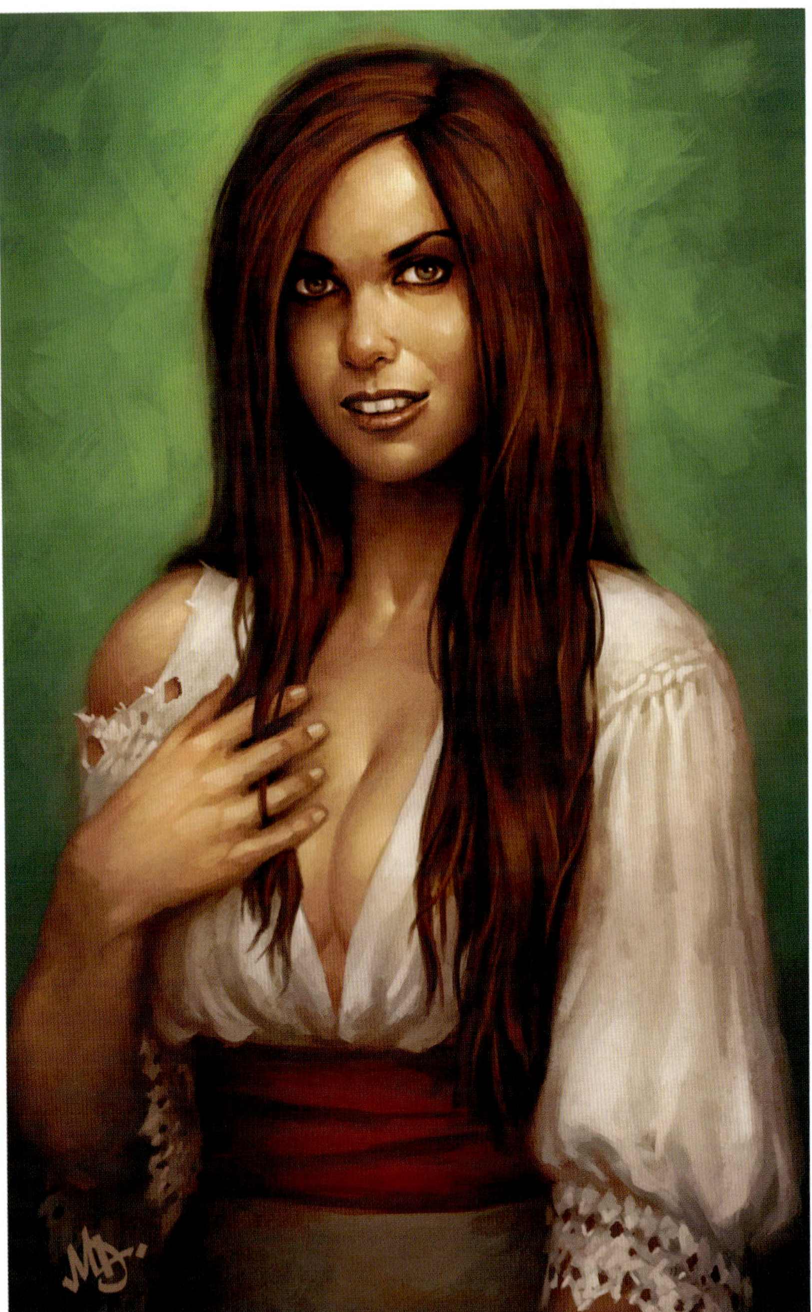

Caroline Munro

On Matt Dixon, Fantasy Illustration, and the Art of Being Fearless

I've always loved art. Growing up, long before my dyslexia was diagnosed so the teachers just referred to me as being "slow", art and sport were the only subjects I was really any good at while everything else was very much of a muddle. Thinking back to those years at The Old Vicarage School in Richmond, the only teacher I really remember is Miss Moore, the young art mistress who was a great inspiration and even put one of my pictures forward for a local competition. It was displayed in the window of Bentalls department store in Kingston upon Thames. I won a packet of Rowney crayons for my effort.

When we moved down to the south coast of England and I was schooled at St Martha's Convent in Rottingdean, the nuns were less inspirational. Although my work suffered I still managed to scrape an O–level pass. It was the only exam I took because the nuns made it clear that there was no point bothering with the rest. Although it was a big relief to me then, it turned out that I wouldn't have enough qualifications to meet the basic requirements to enroll at the Brighton College of Arts and Crafts. Luckily I was allowed to enroll for their Saturday morning life drawing classes. One weekend a photography student asked if I would model for him and after one of the pictures, taken in the grounds of Preston Manor, was entered in The Evening News' "search for a new model" contest, my life took a whole different path.

So instead of creating my own art I've been left to appreciate the work of others, which brings me to Matt. Even before we get to the subject matter let me just say how much I love his use of colour and light, especially the purples and greens, which are my favourite colours. When it comes to the characters, it's easy for fantasy artists to objectify the women they create, exaggerating their proportions to the extreme. Matt doesn't do that. Though the wonderful women in his paintings may range from impish little things to sturdy warriors, from the macabre to the more carefree, while they have an air of mischief around them they still look like they can handle themselves. It's this confidence and strength of character that runs throughout his paintings. Sexy and beautiful, it's the eyes that best illustrate their strong personality. Look at Matt's paintings and you know in an instant that here are characters in control of their own destinies.

I learnt early on in my modelling days that eye contact was the most important thing because it draws the audience in, and for that you need to be absolutely fearless. In Matt's work it empowers and emboldens his characters. For that I say, "Well done, Matt!"

Caroline Munro,
London, April 2012

Caroline Munro
Signed up to the Lucie Clayton agency after being chosen as "The Face of 1966" by London's The Evening News, Caroline Munro began her modelling career with a shoot for Vogue before coming to prominence as "Miss Lamb's Navy" in the long–running Lamb's Navy Rum campaign. One of the first billboards caught the attention of Hammer Films' Sir James Carreras who signed her up for a year–long contract. Throughout the 1970s, her appearances in films such as *Dracula AD 1972, Captain Kronos Vampire Hunter, The Golden Voyage of Sinbad, At the Earth's Core, The Spy Who Loved Me*, and *Starcrash* led her to be dubbed The First Lady of Fantasy.

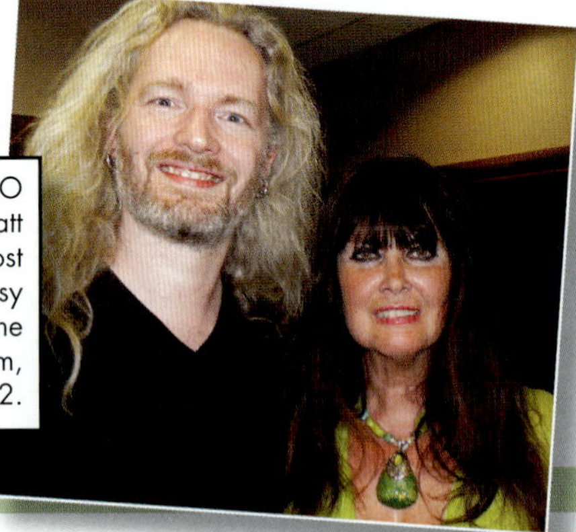

Geek-boy dreams DO come true, as Matt meets one of his most important fantasy art muses, Caroline Munro, in Birmingham, England, March 2012.

For the latest updates, go to: www.mattdixon.co.uk

Girls on Top 2
More Pin-Up Art of Matt Dixon

Book design by Grassy Knoll Studios.

Published by SQP Inc.
PO Box 248 - Columbus NJ 08022

Sal Quartuccio & Bob Keenan - Publishers

For a free, full color catalog a showcasing the entire SQP line of erotic, fantasy, and pin-up artwork, go to:
www.sqpartbooks.com

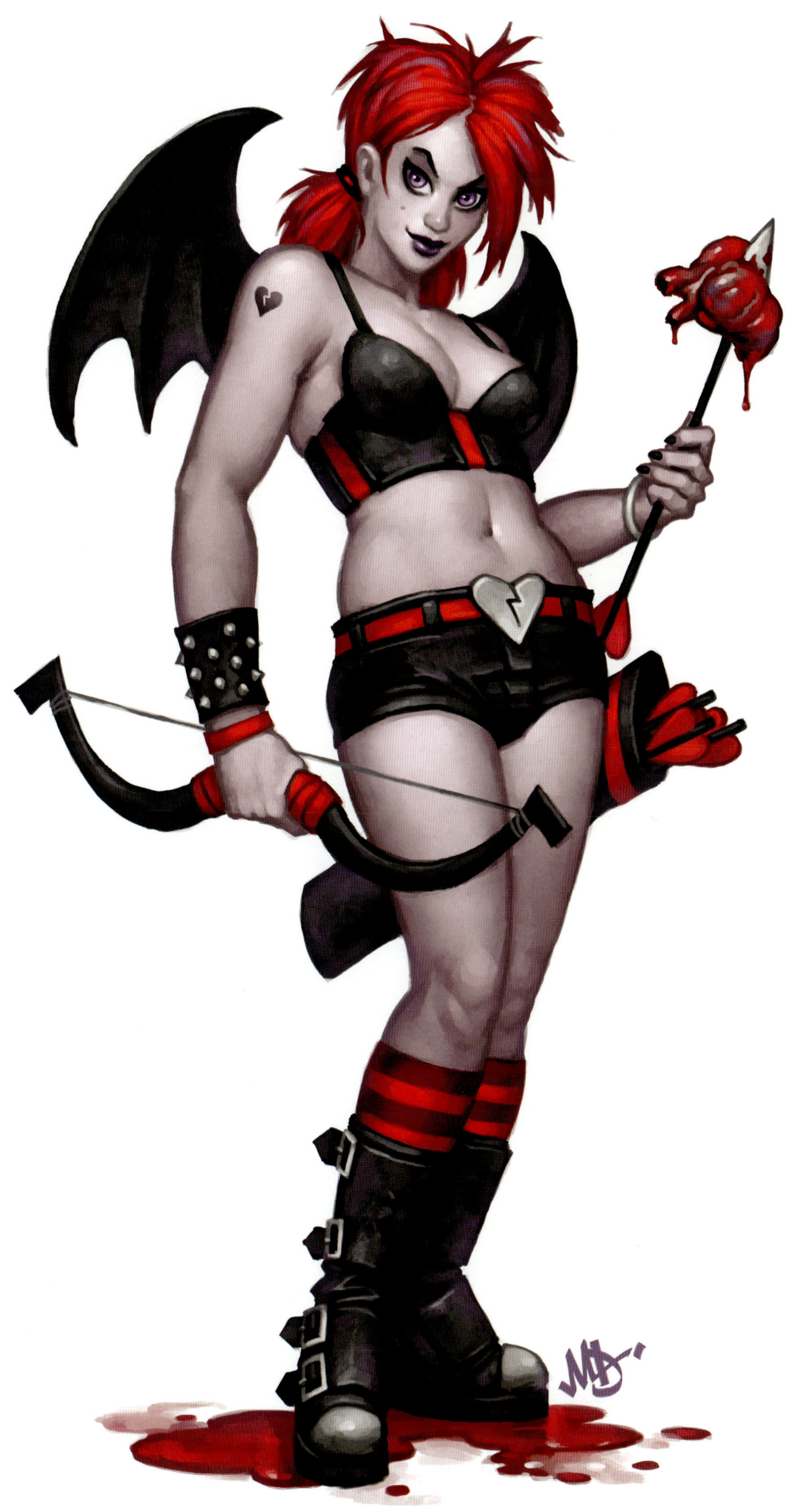

Bad Cupid

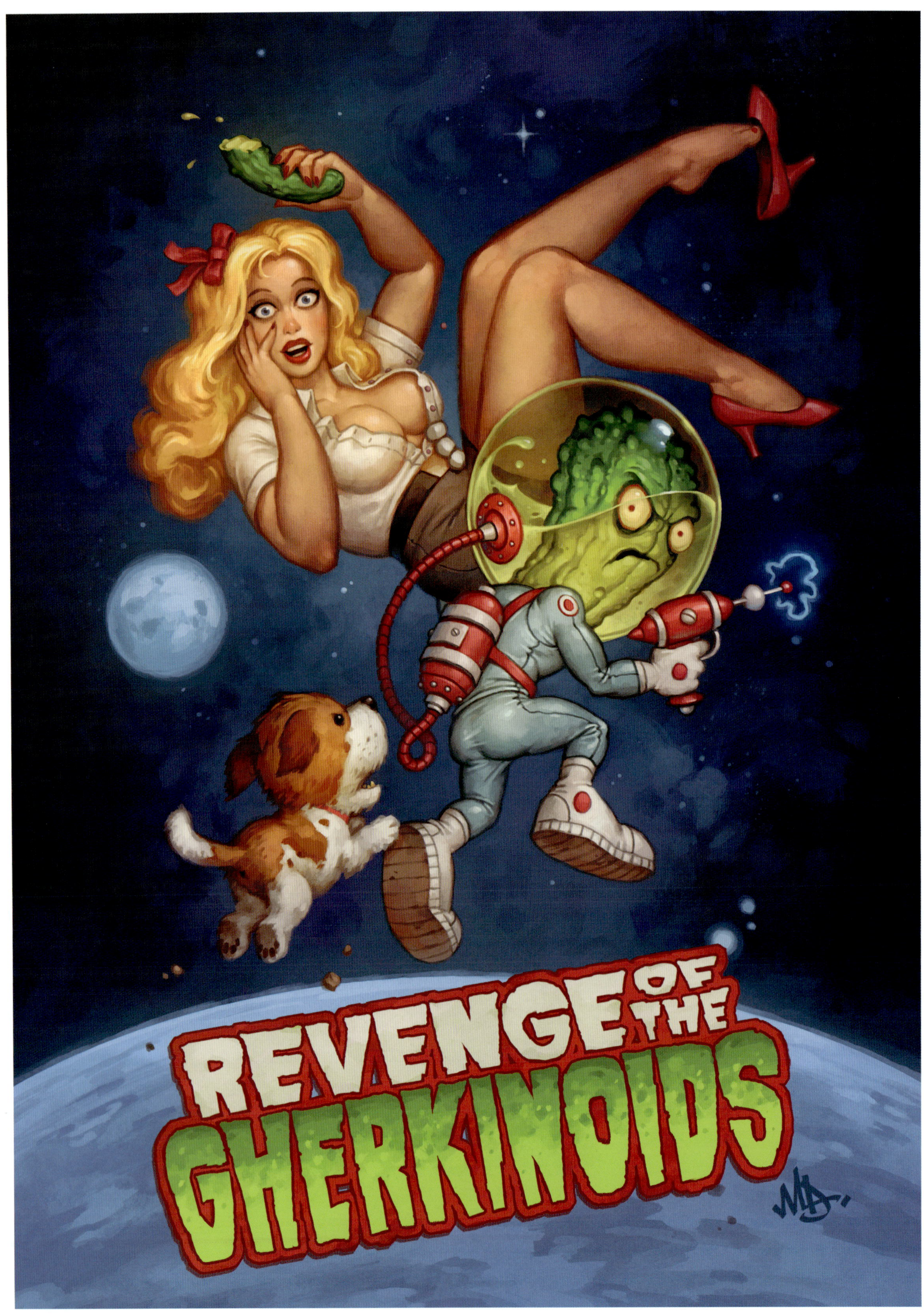

Revenge of the Gherkinoids

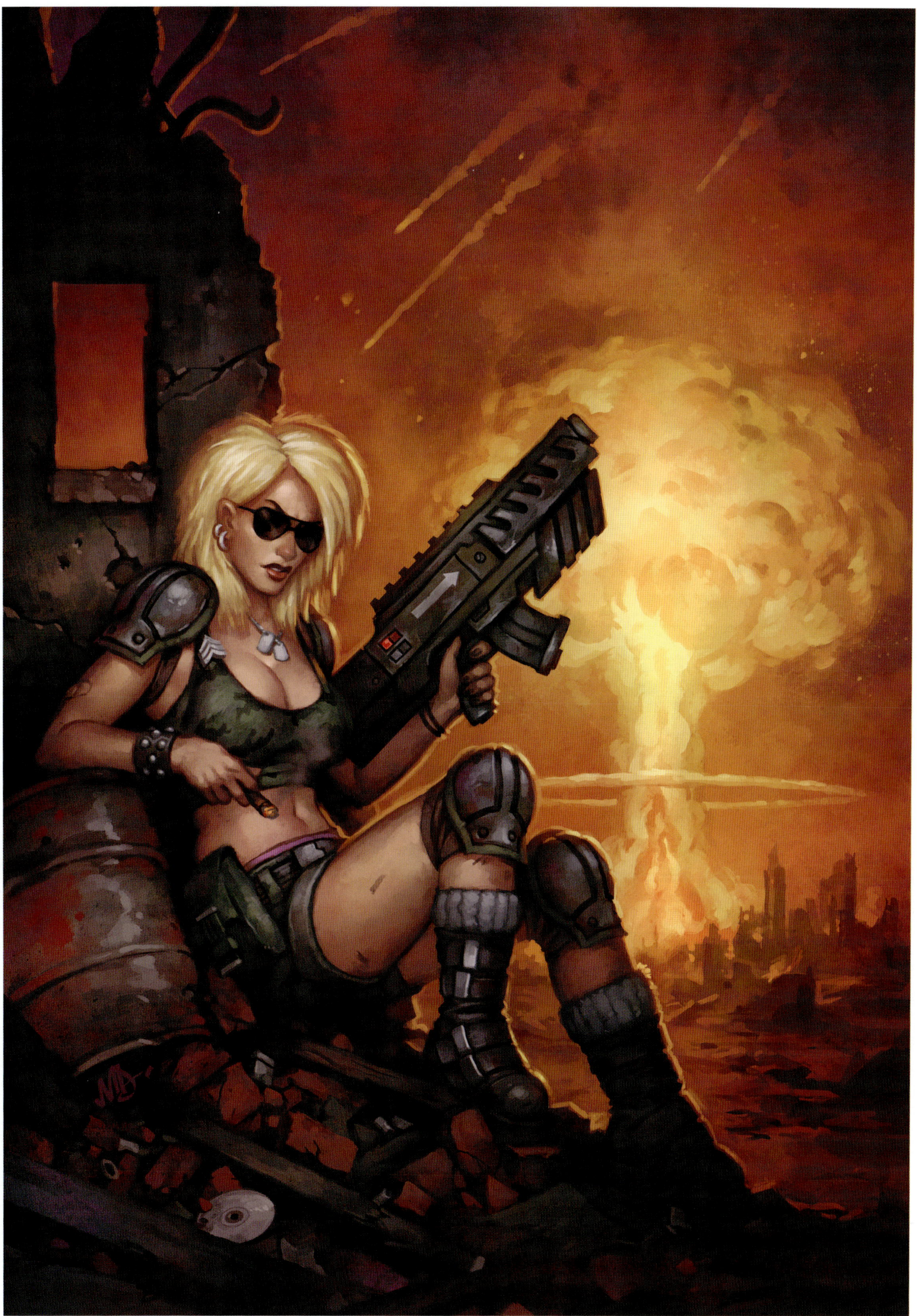

Endgame

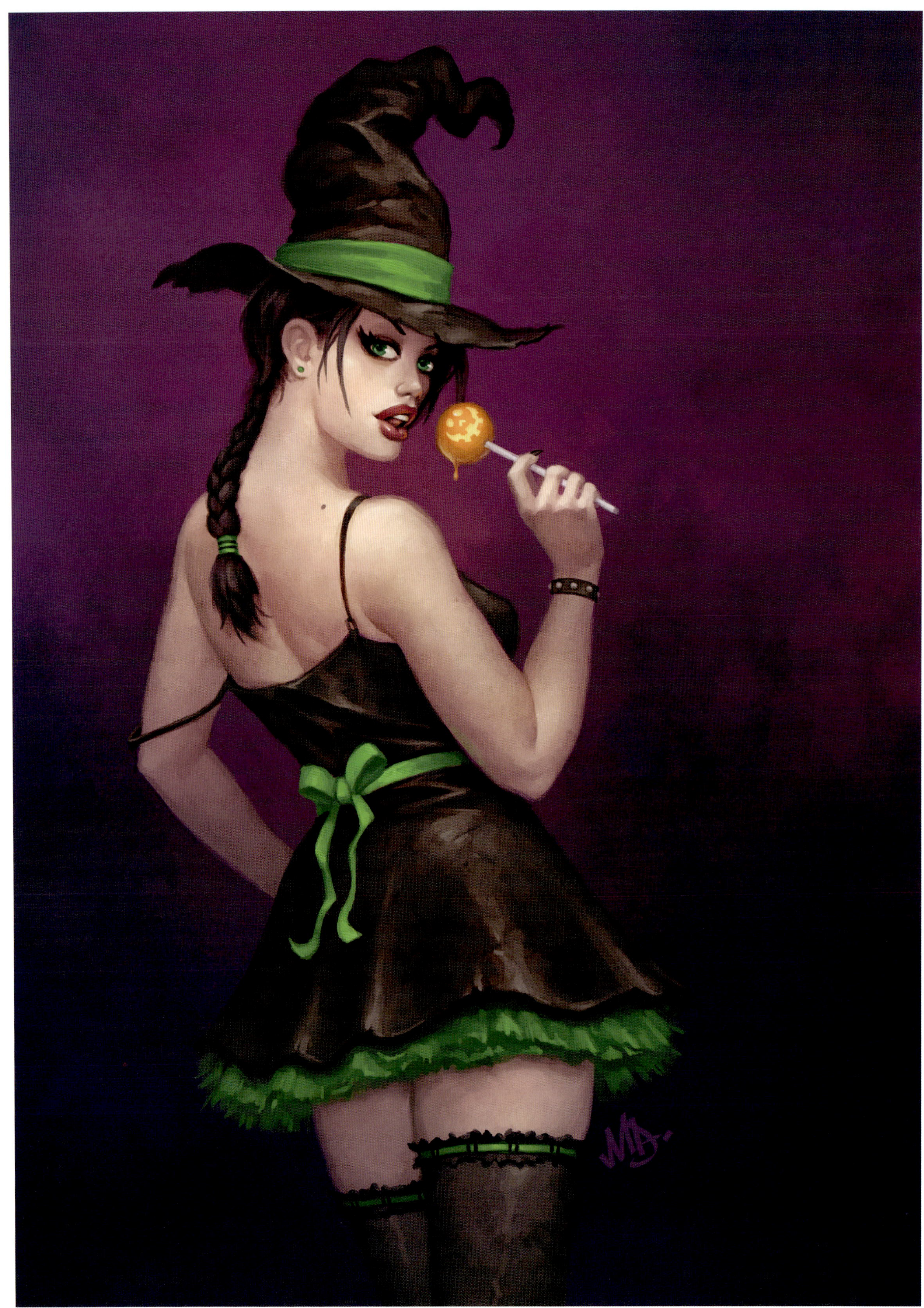

Pumpkin Candy

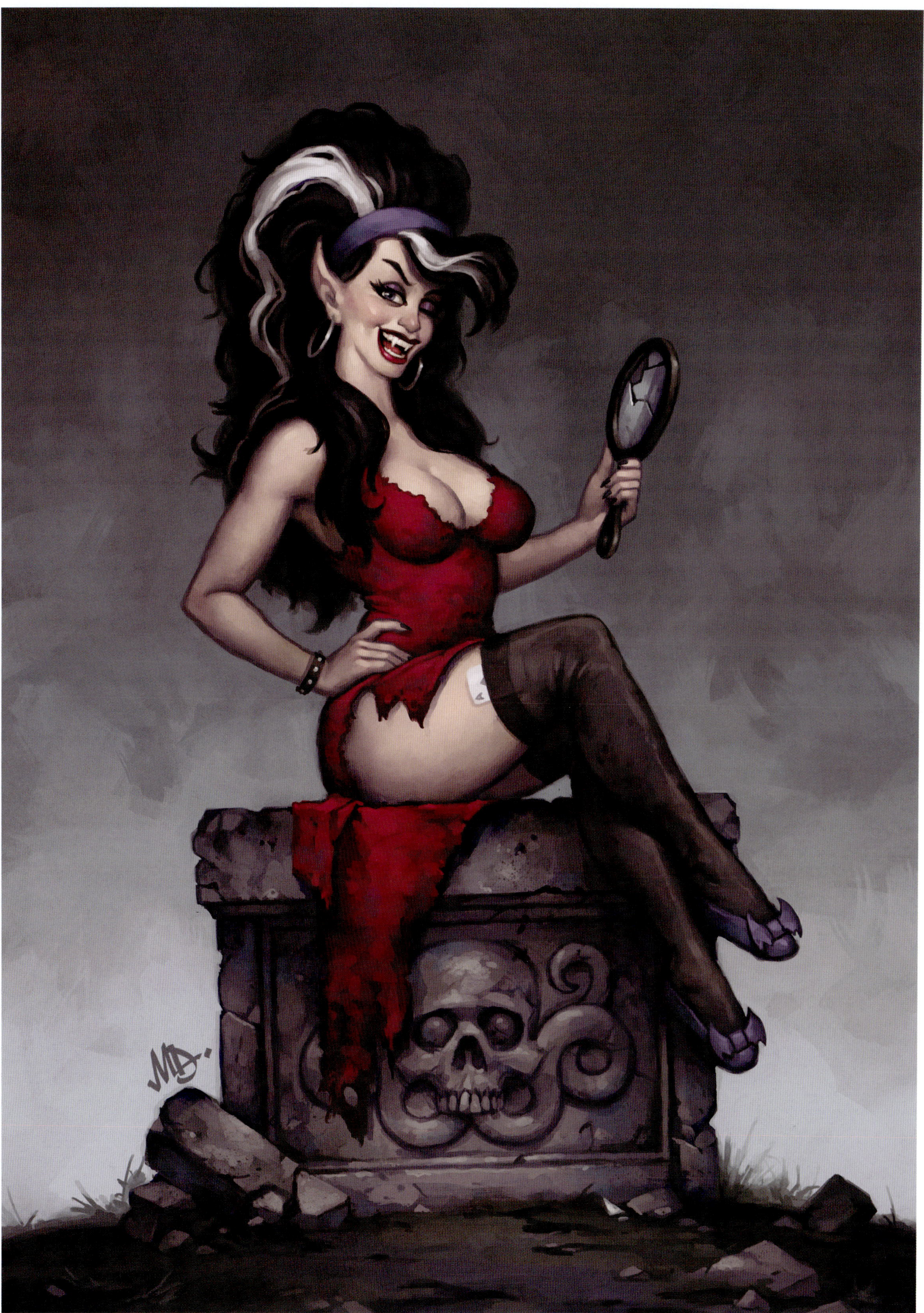

All In Vein

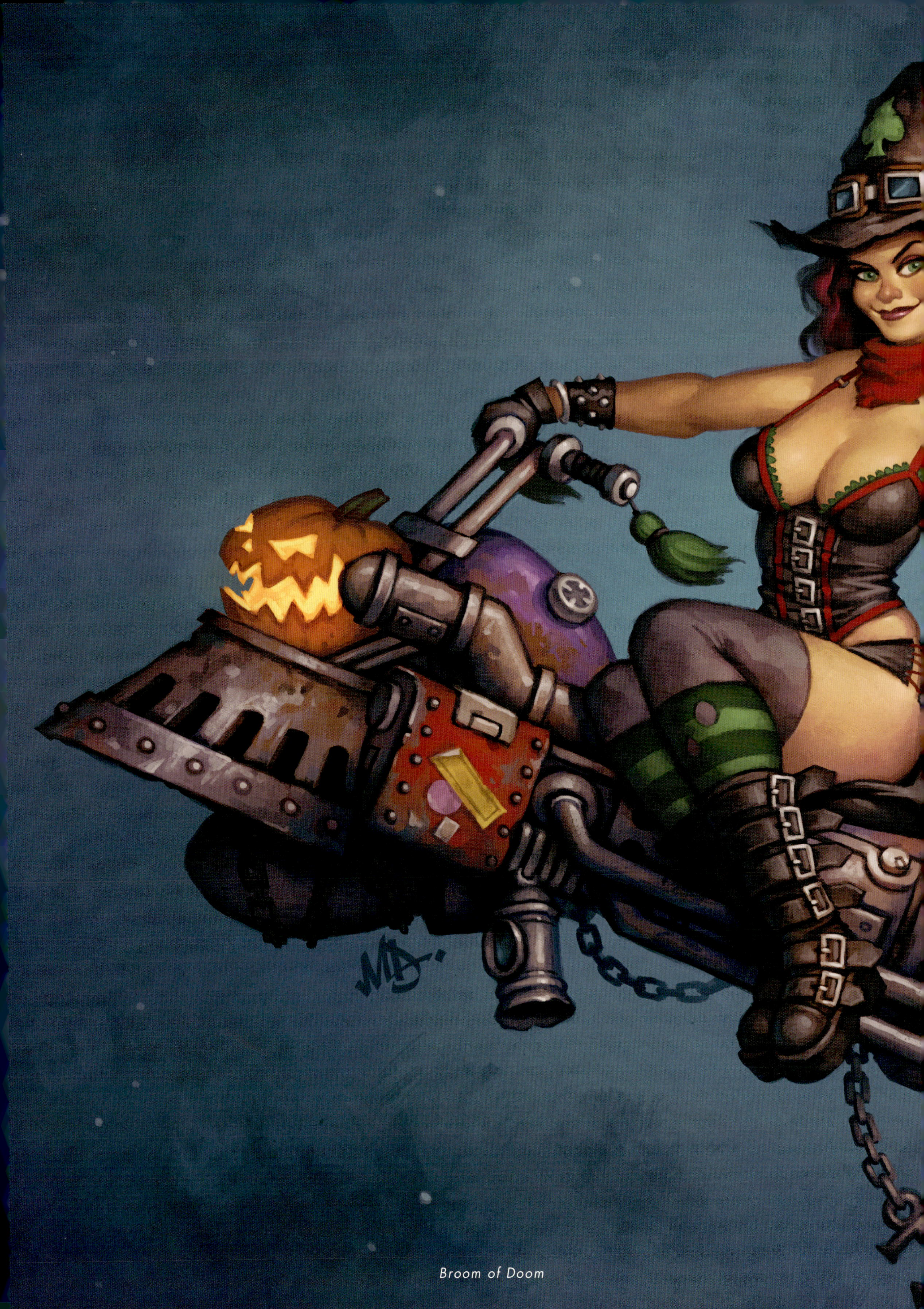

Broom of Doom

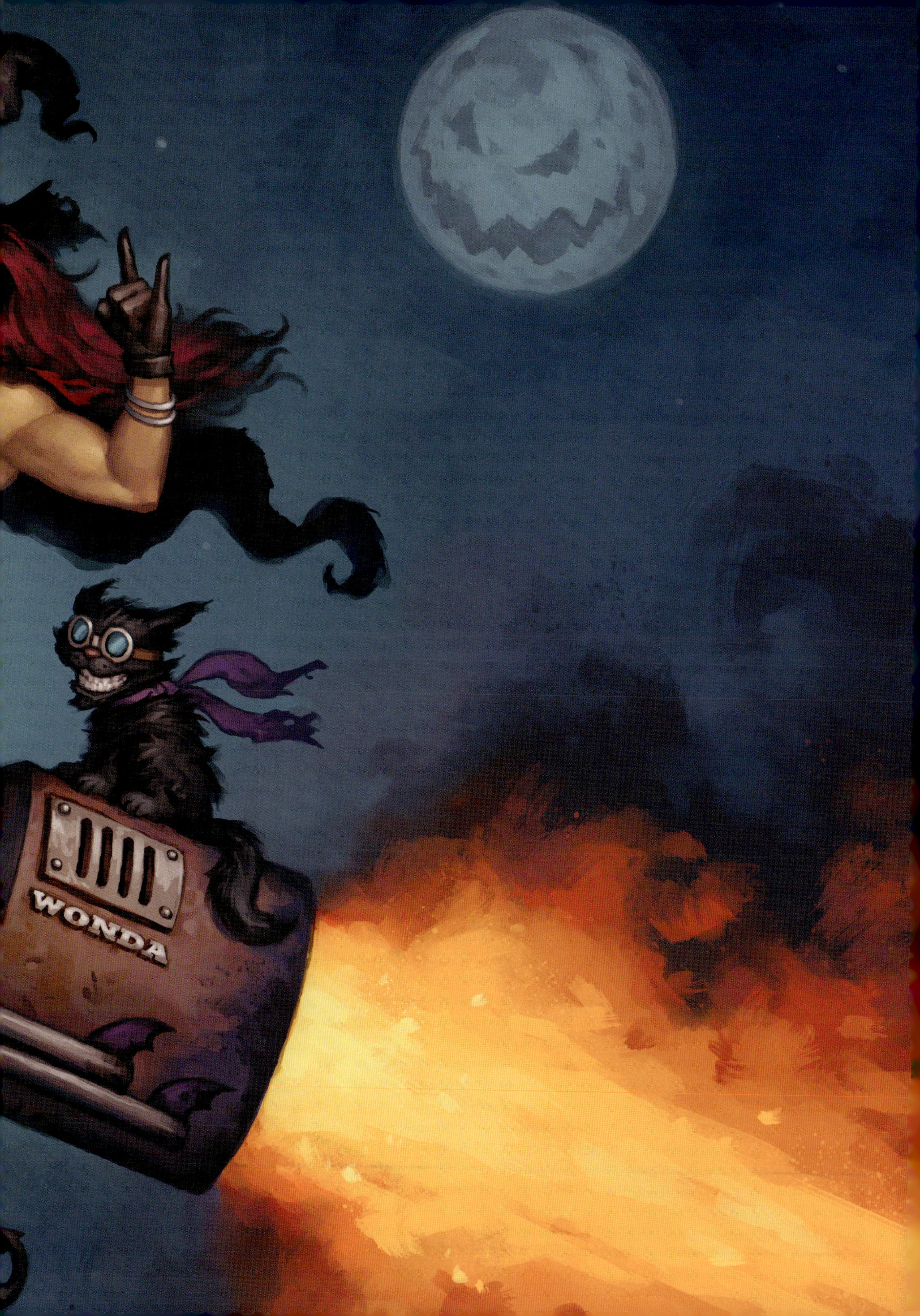
WONDA

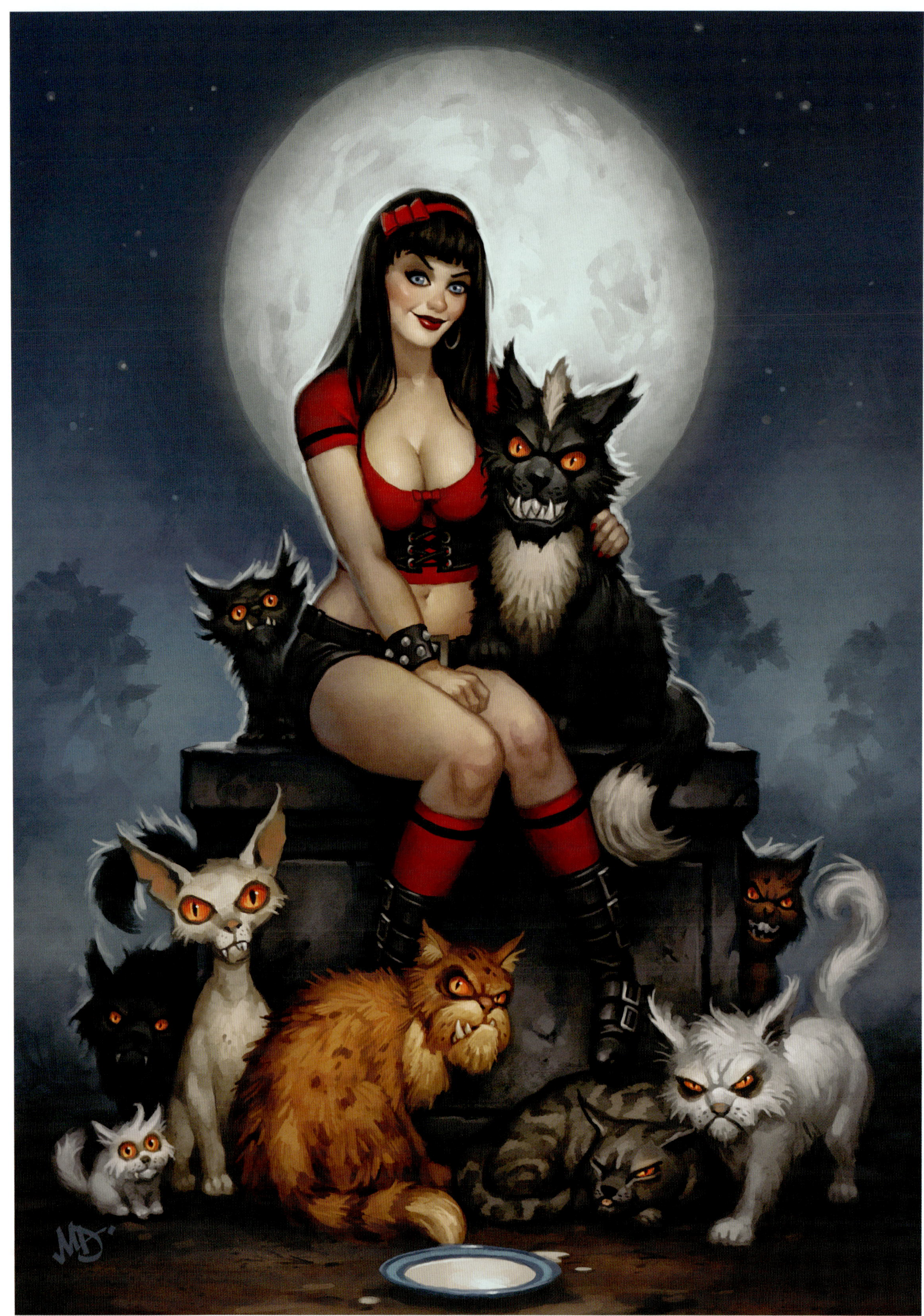

Moon Milk

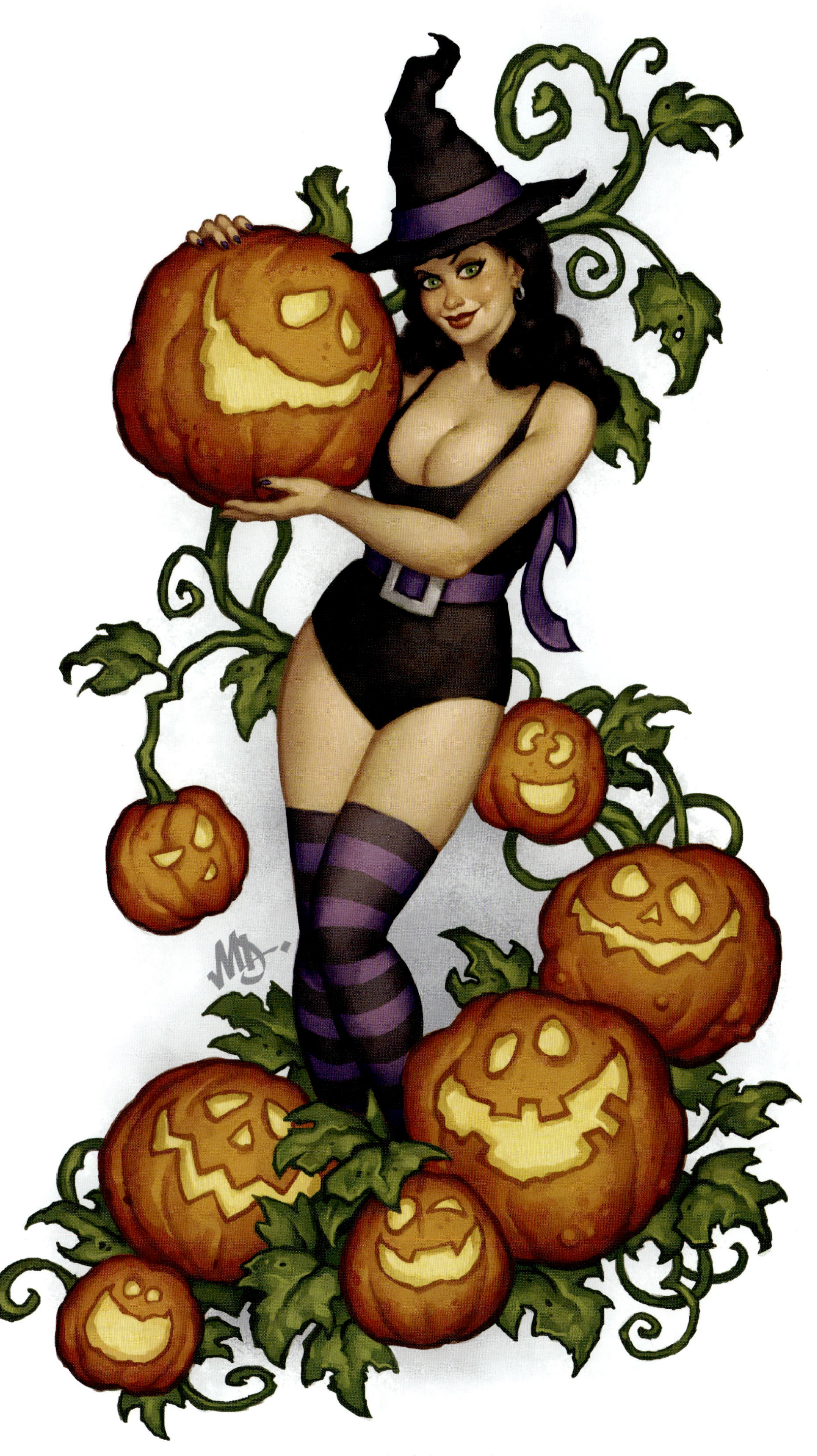

Pick of the Patch

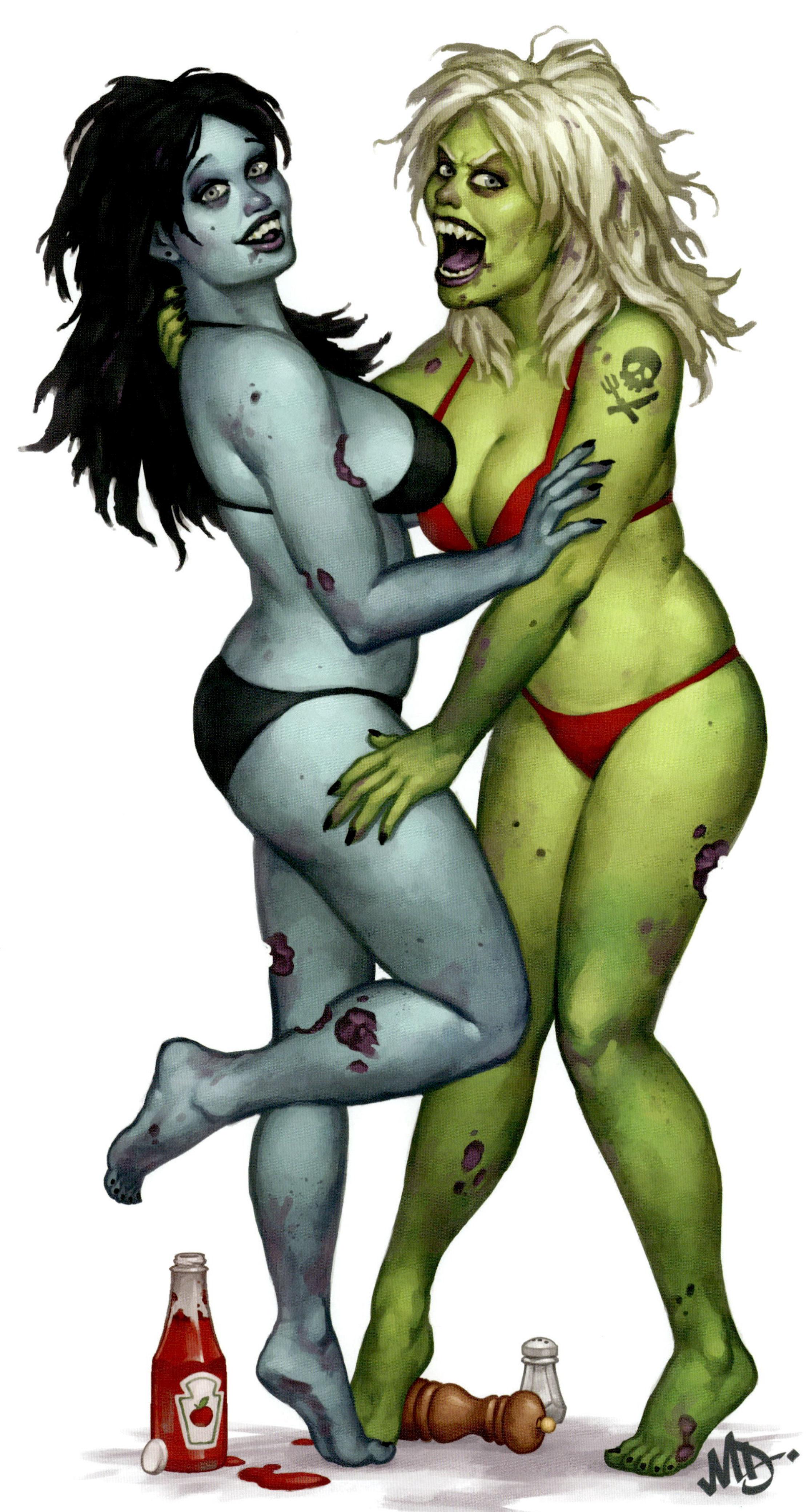

Love Bites

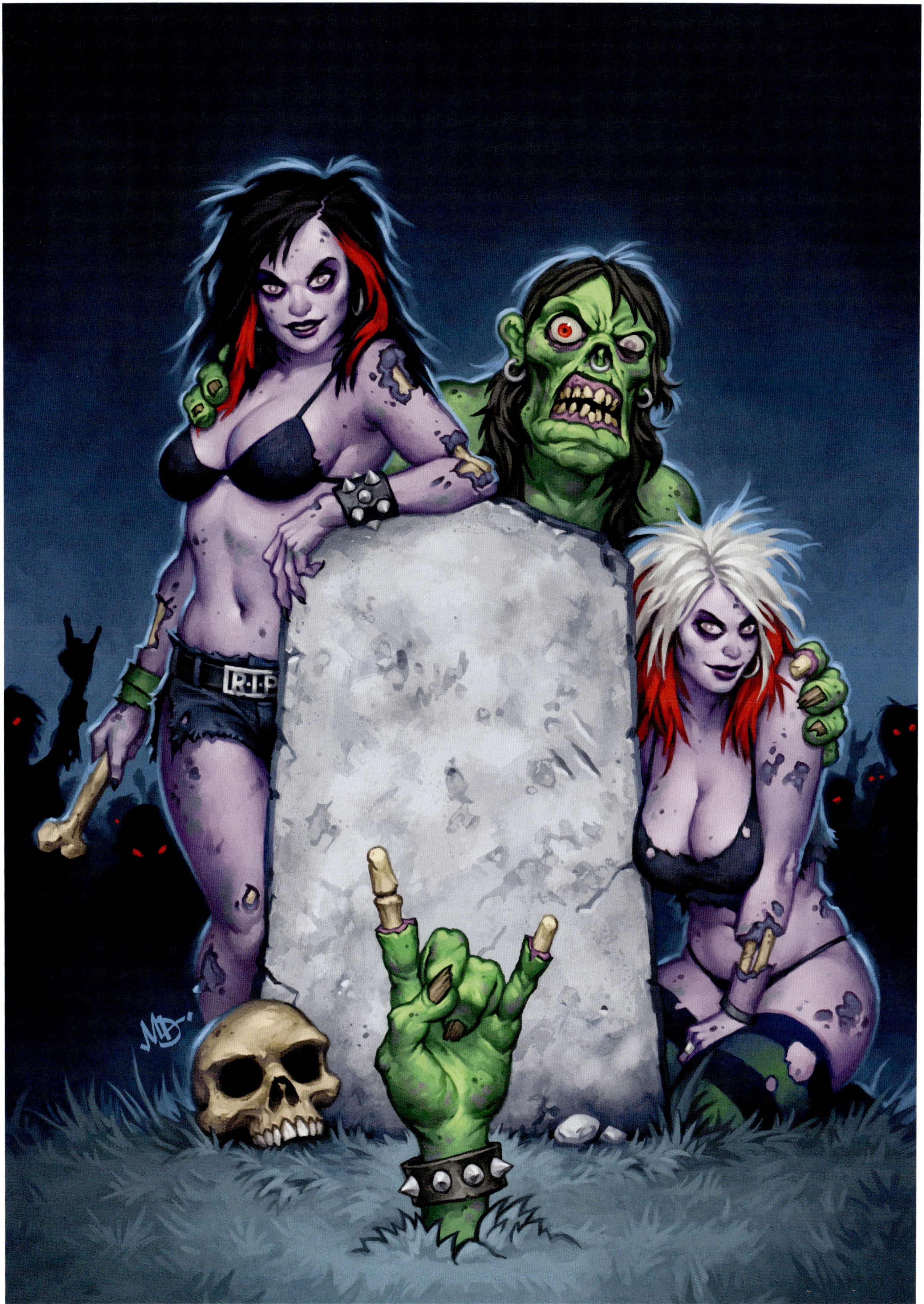

Zombies Rock

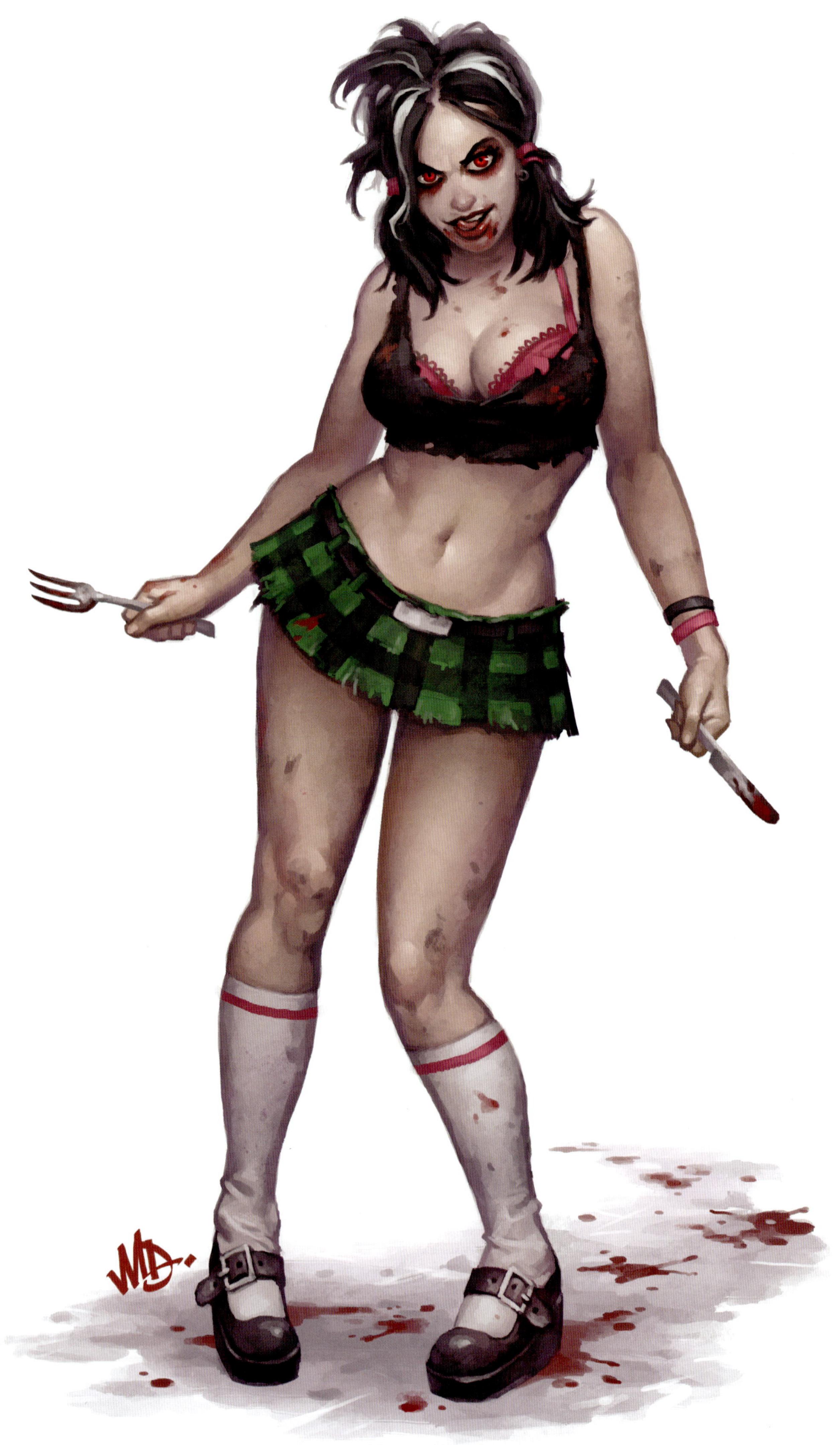

Hungry Hanna

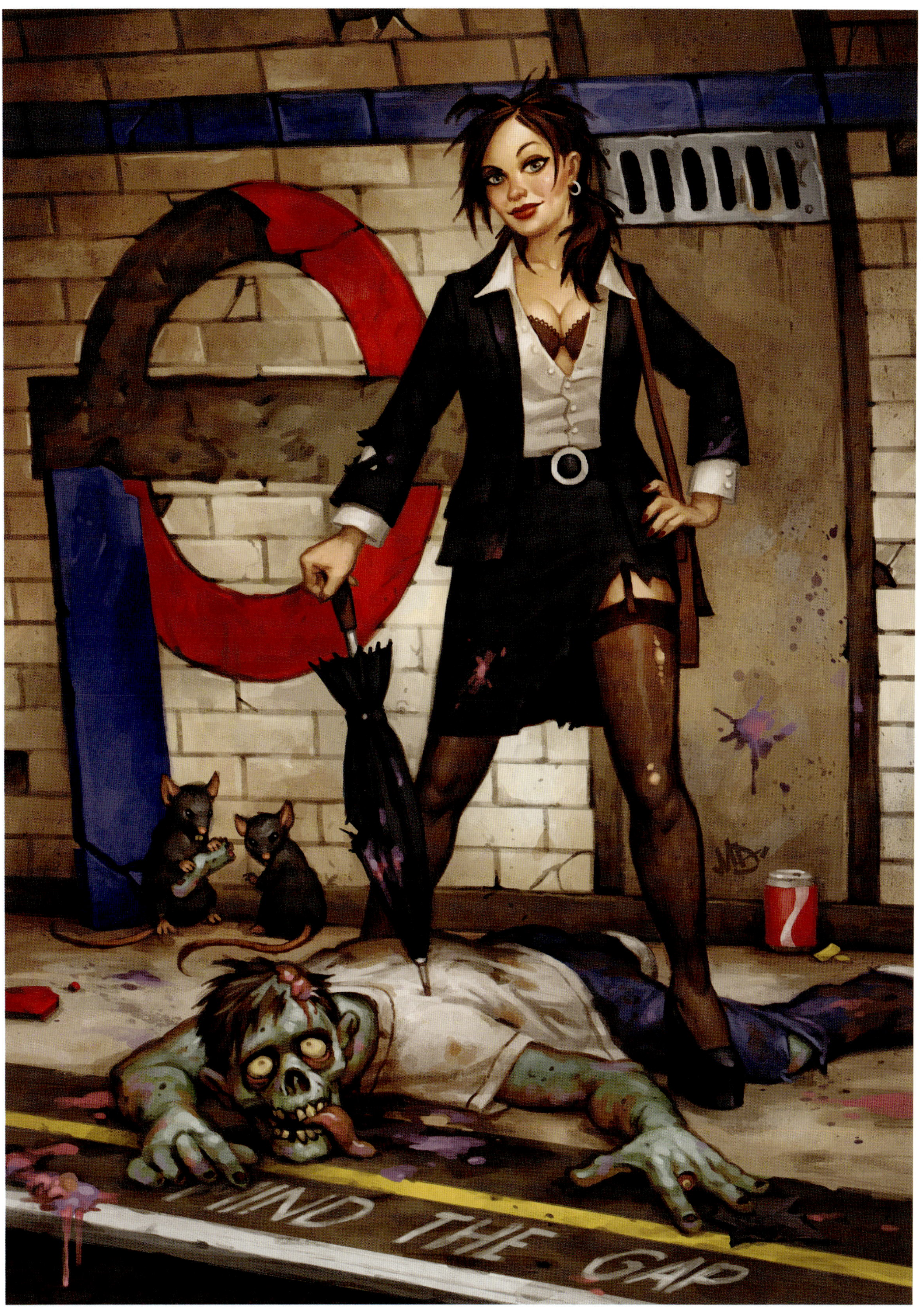

Tube Zombie
www.londonhorrorcomic.com

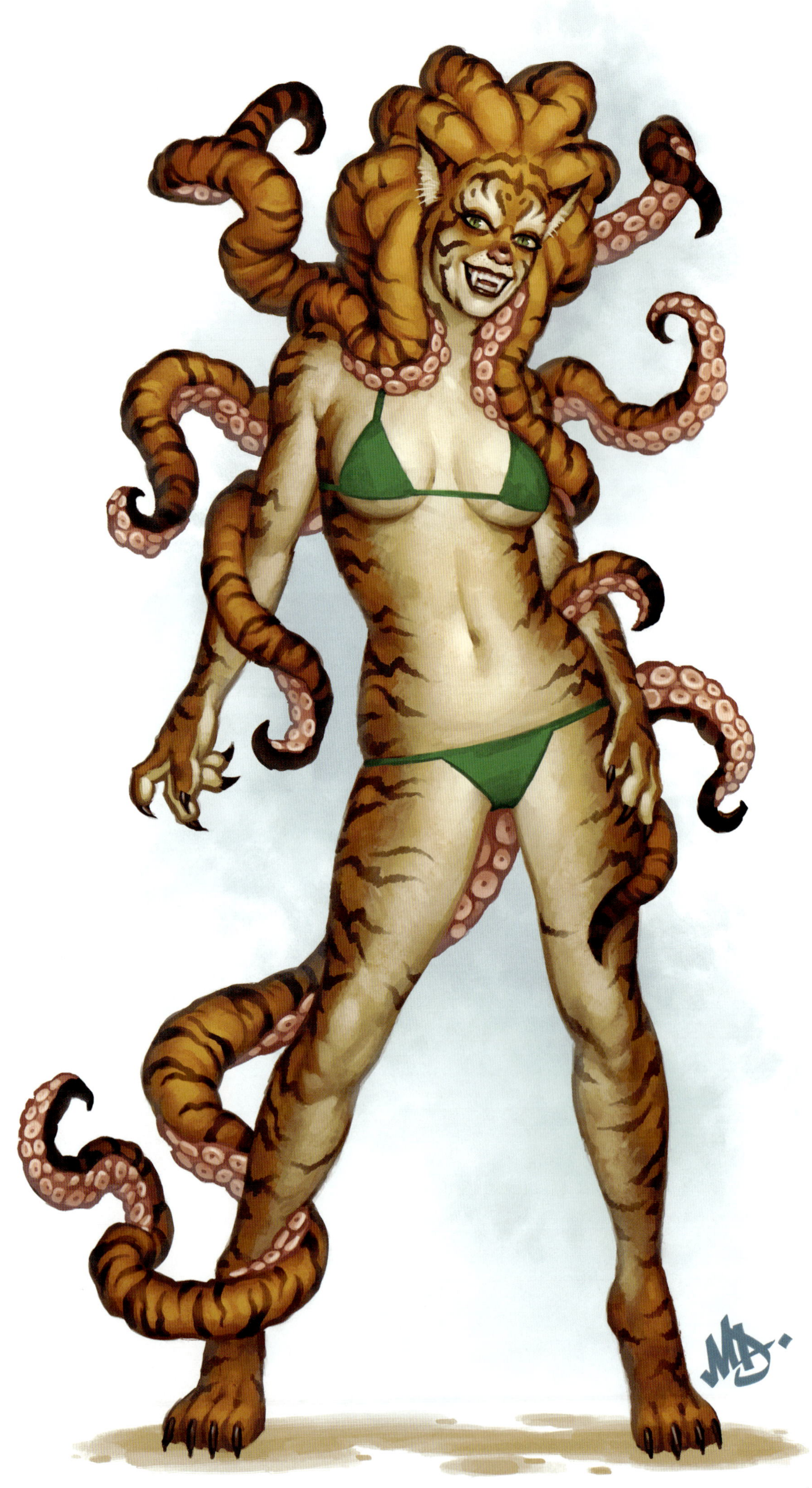

Sabretoothed Squid Girl

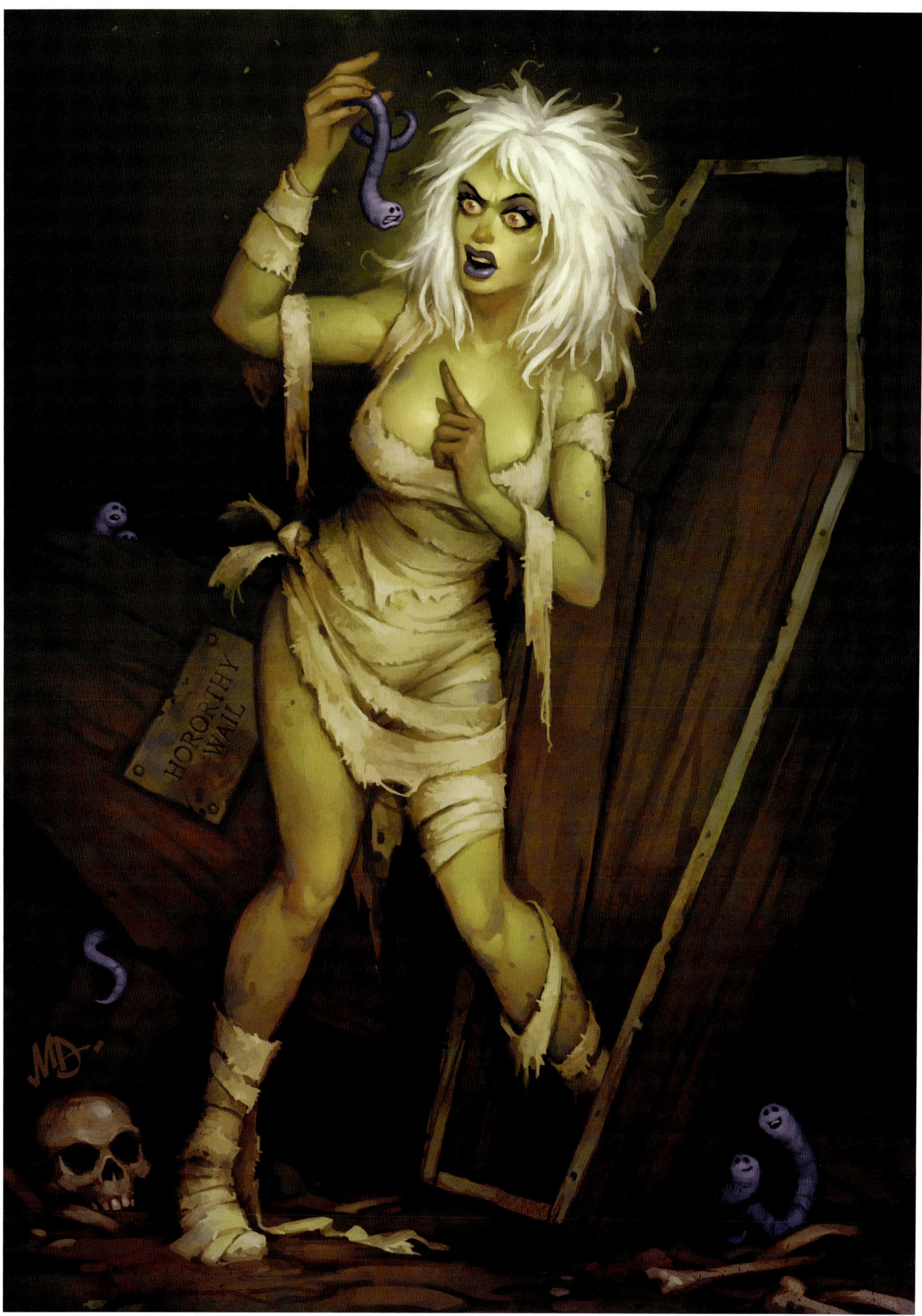

That's Not for Nibbling!

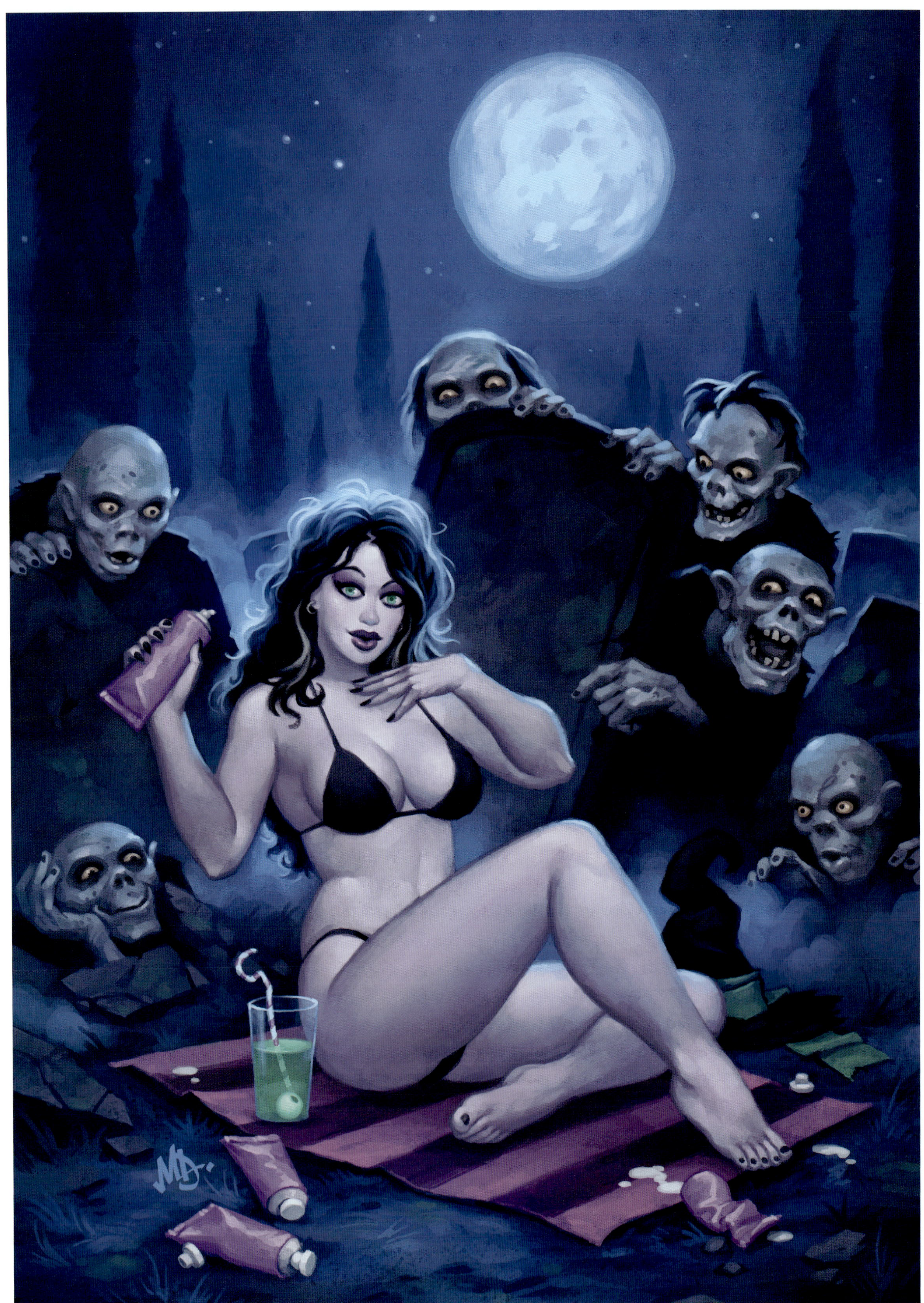

Catching Some Beams

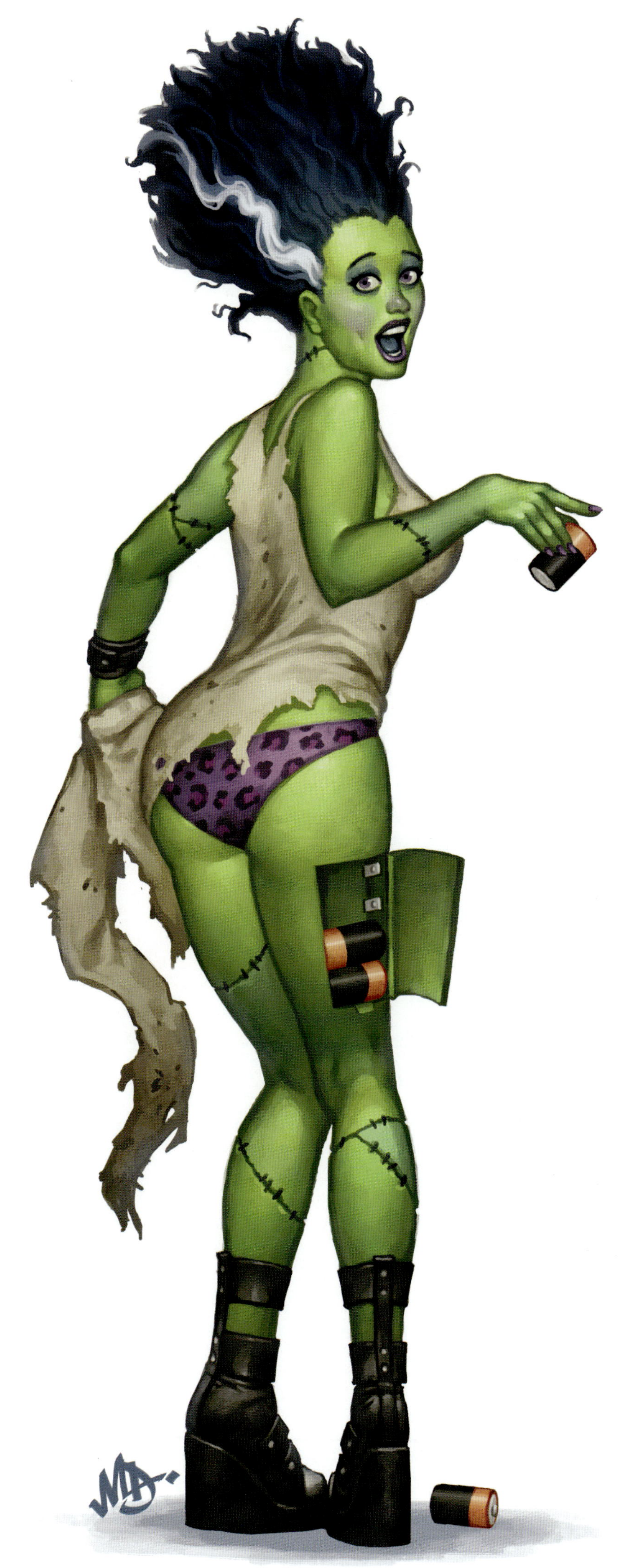

Caught Changing

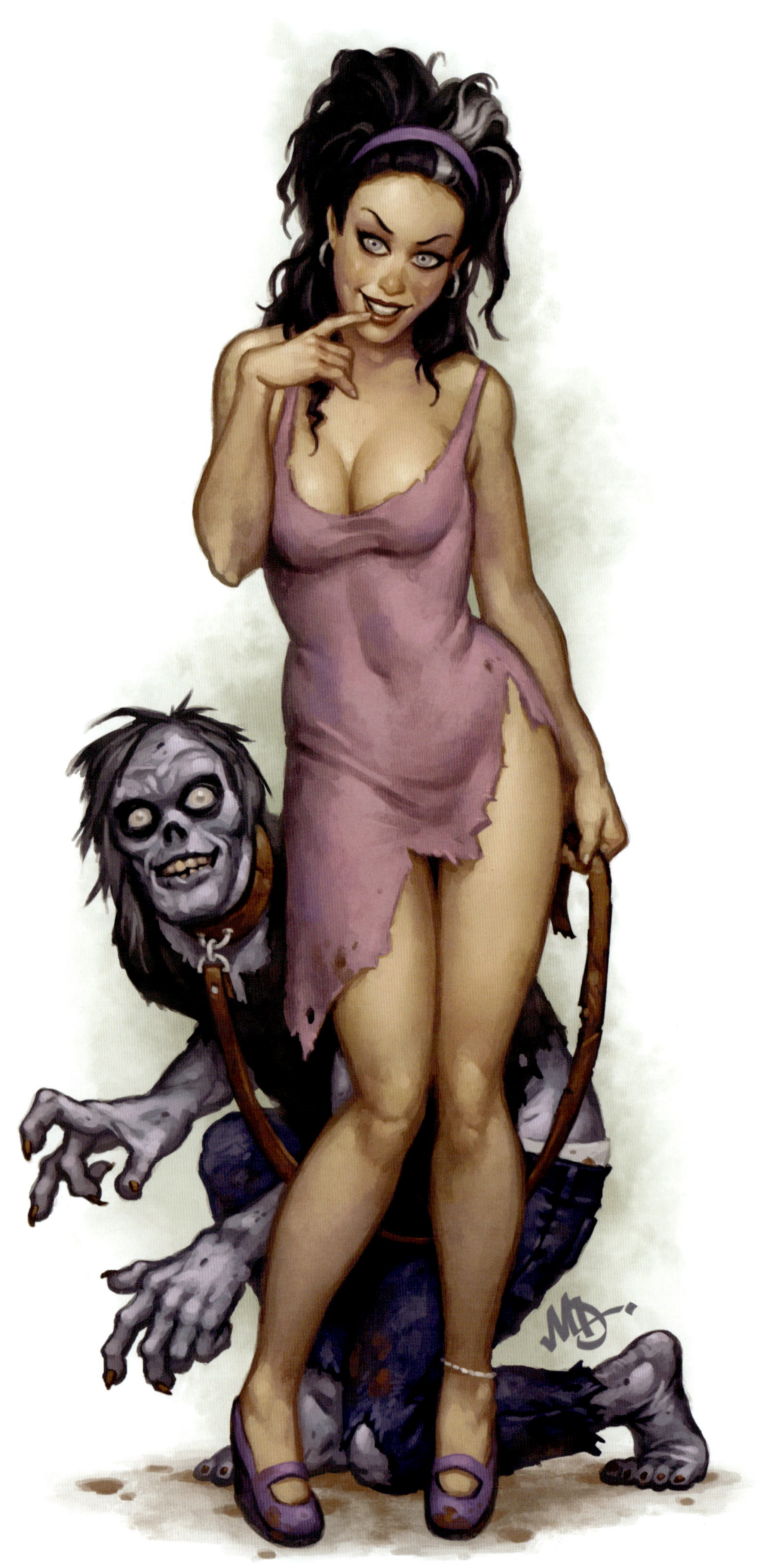

Albert's Outing

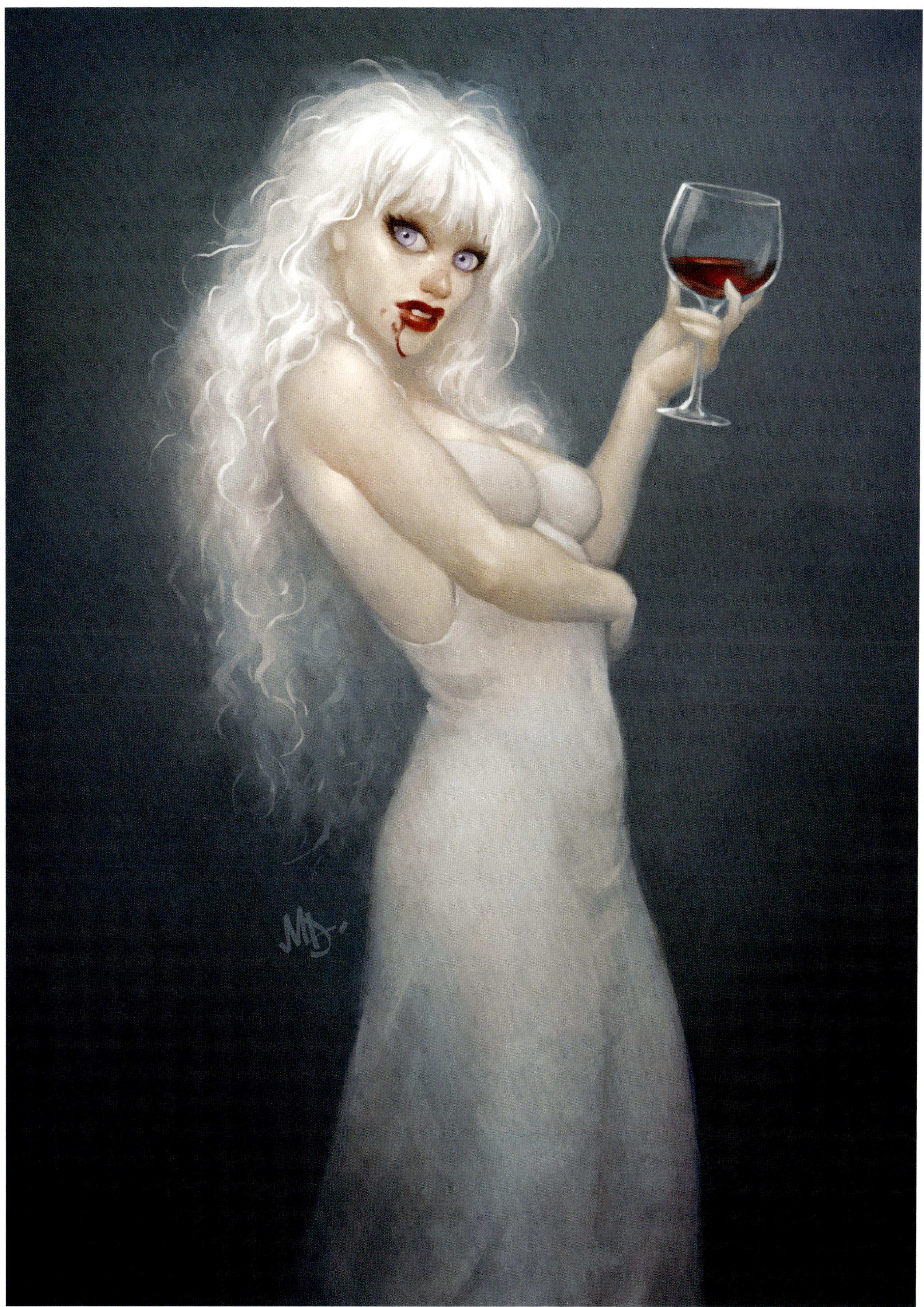

Bloody Mary

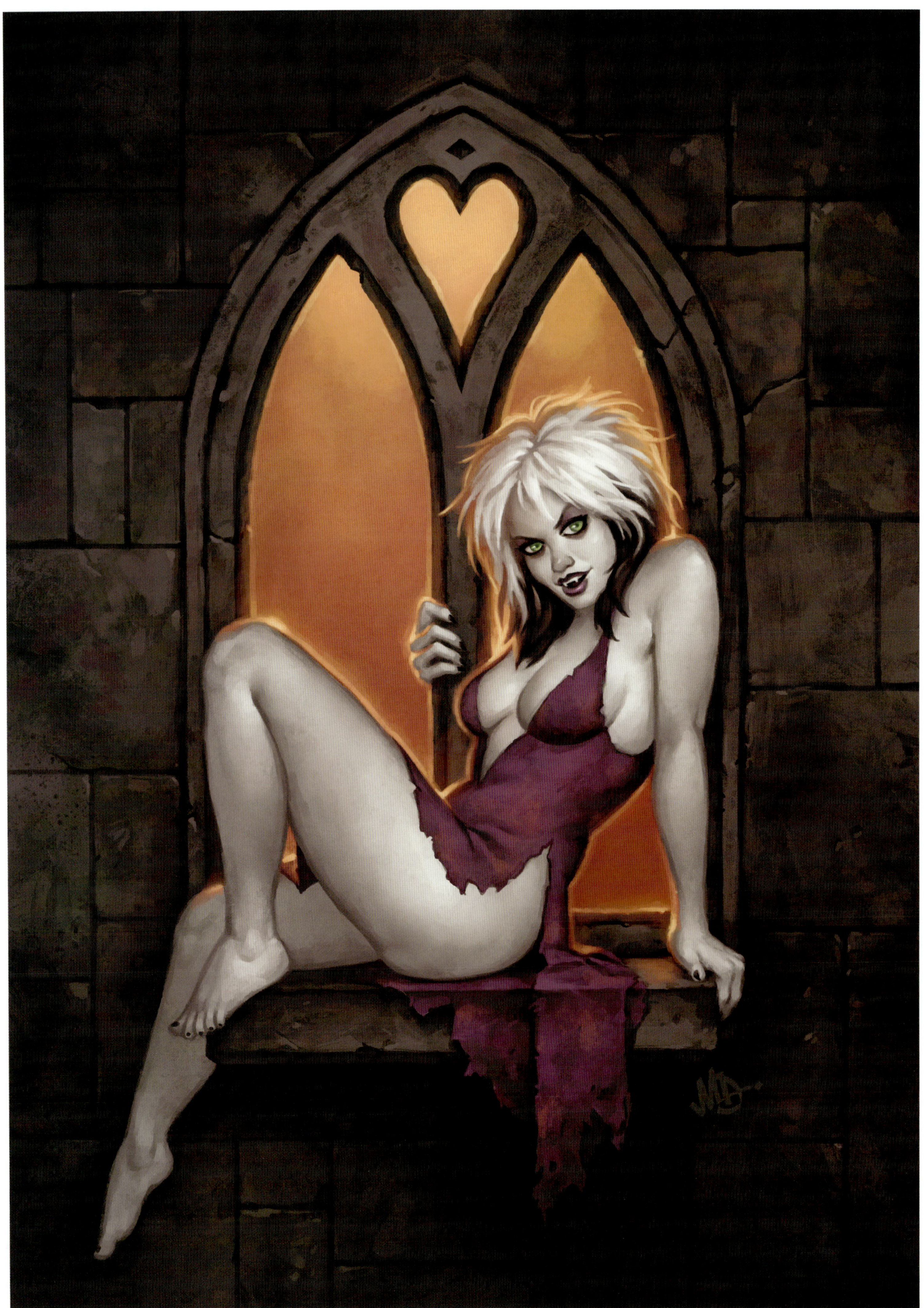

Vespertine

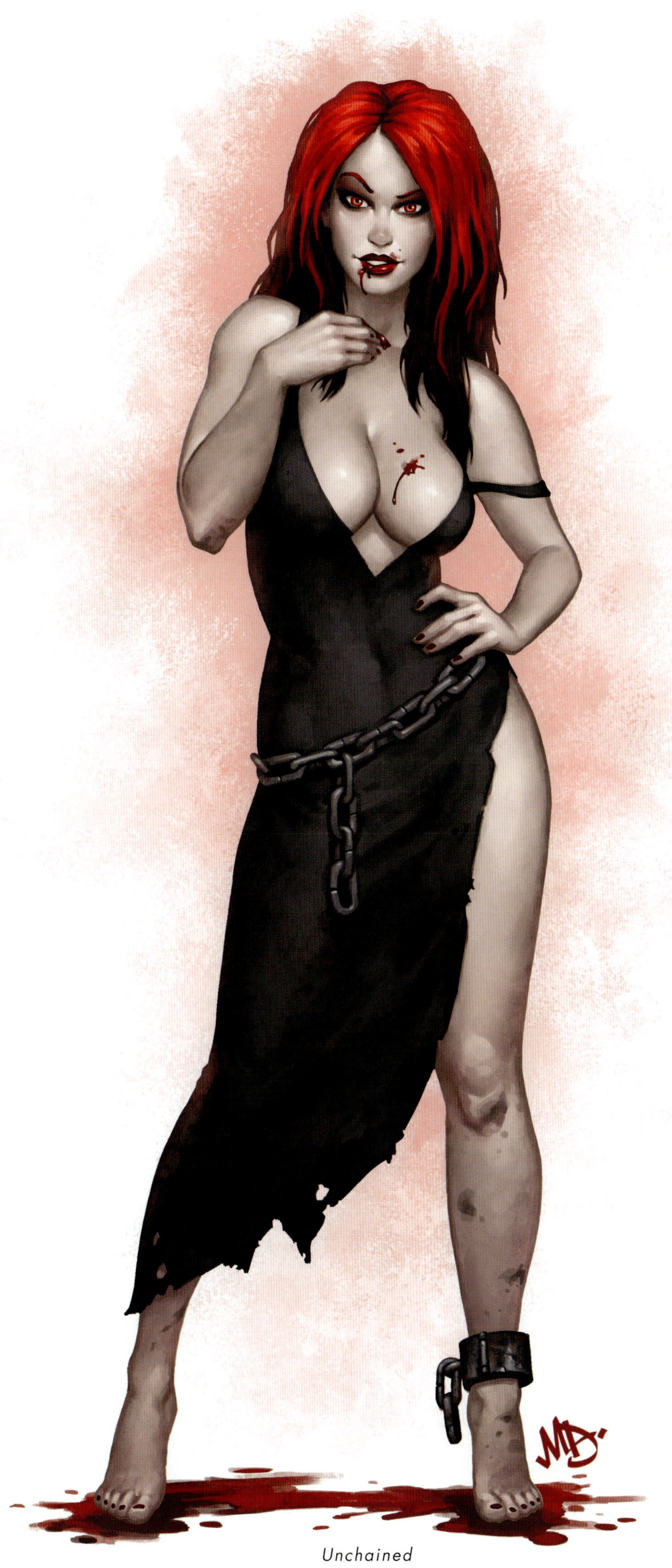

Unchained

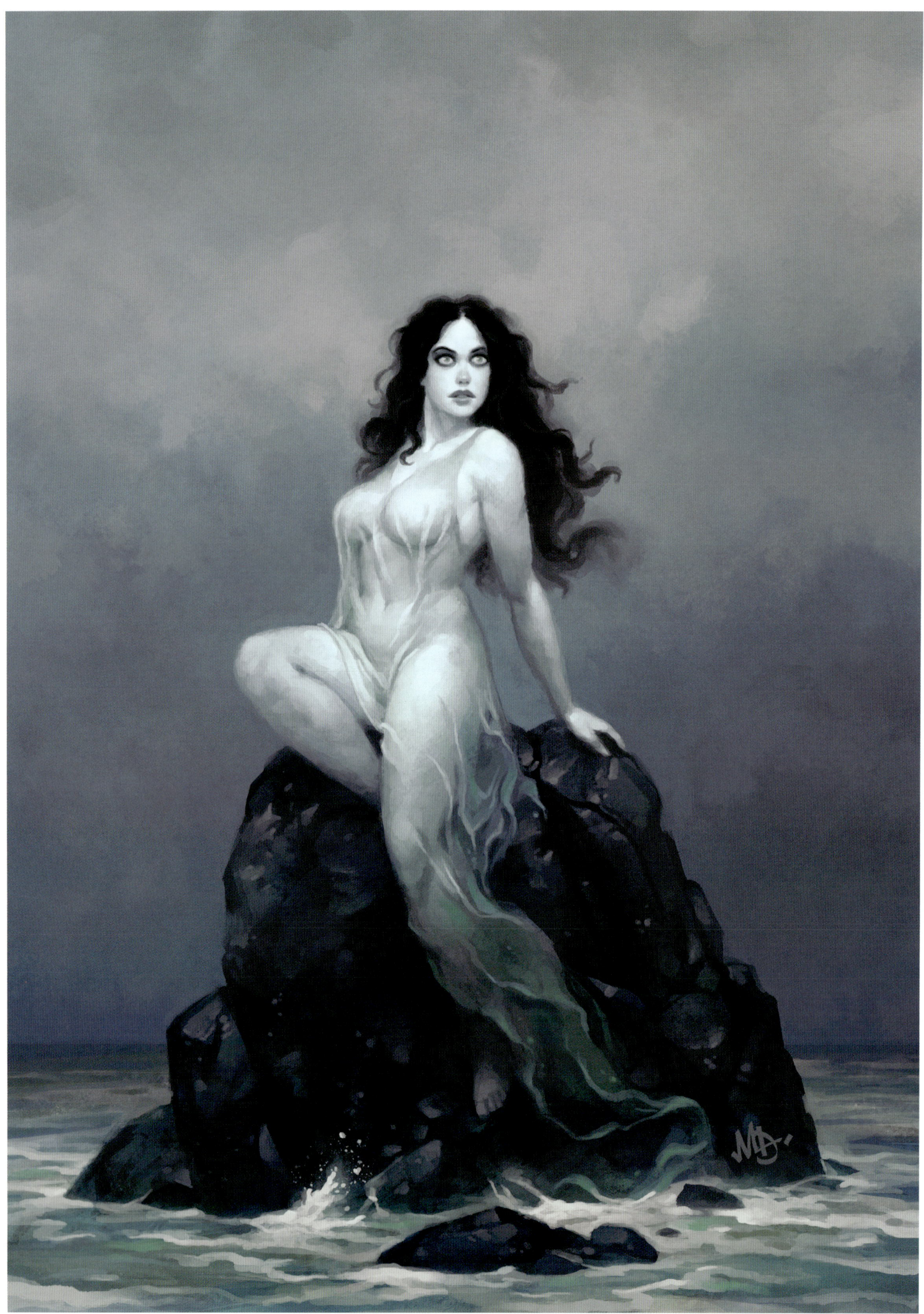

Selkie

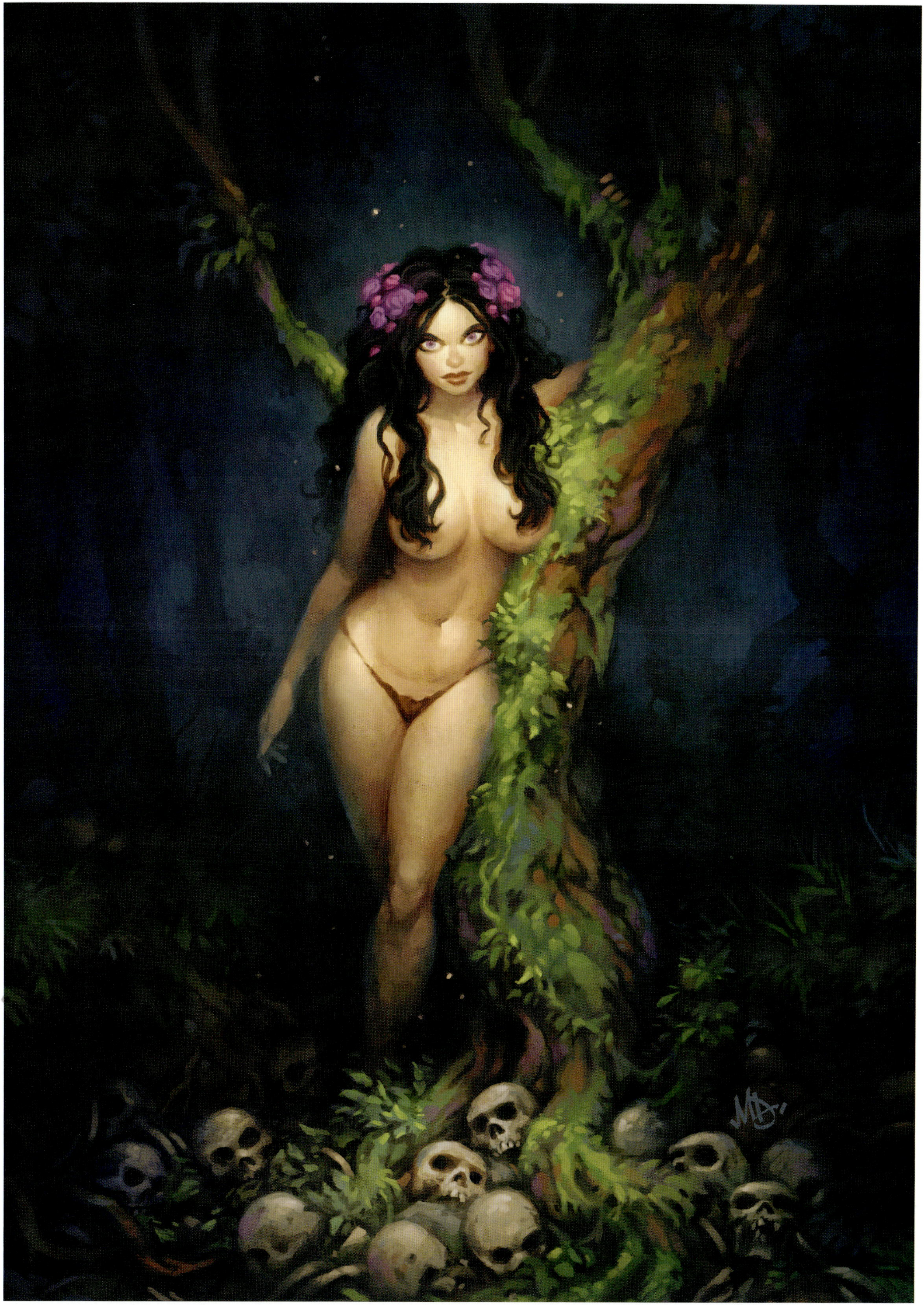

Dryad

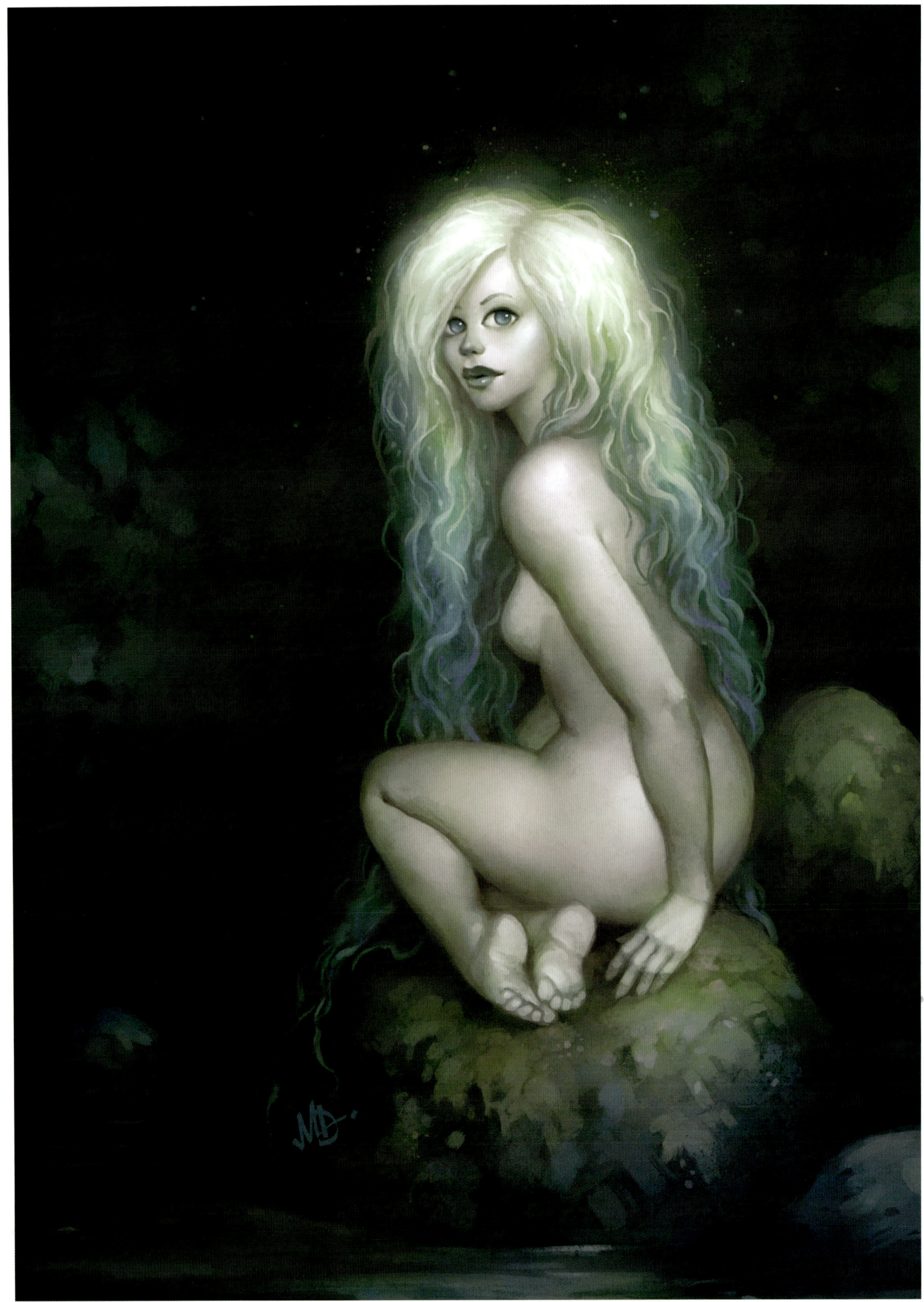

Selene

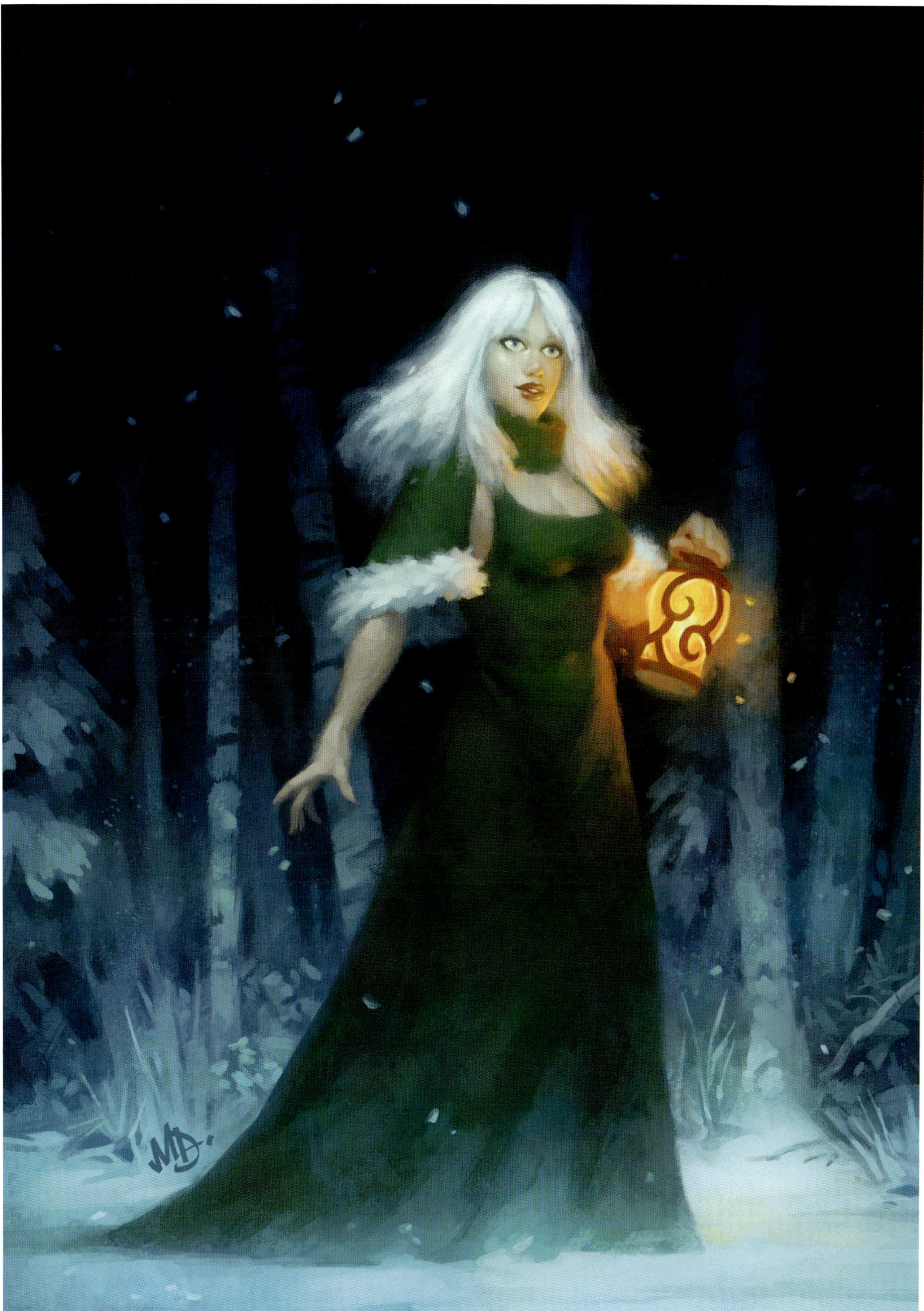

Winter

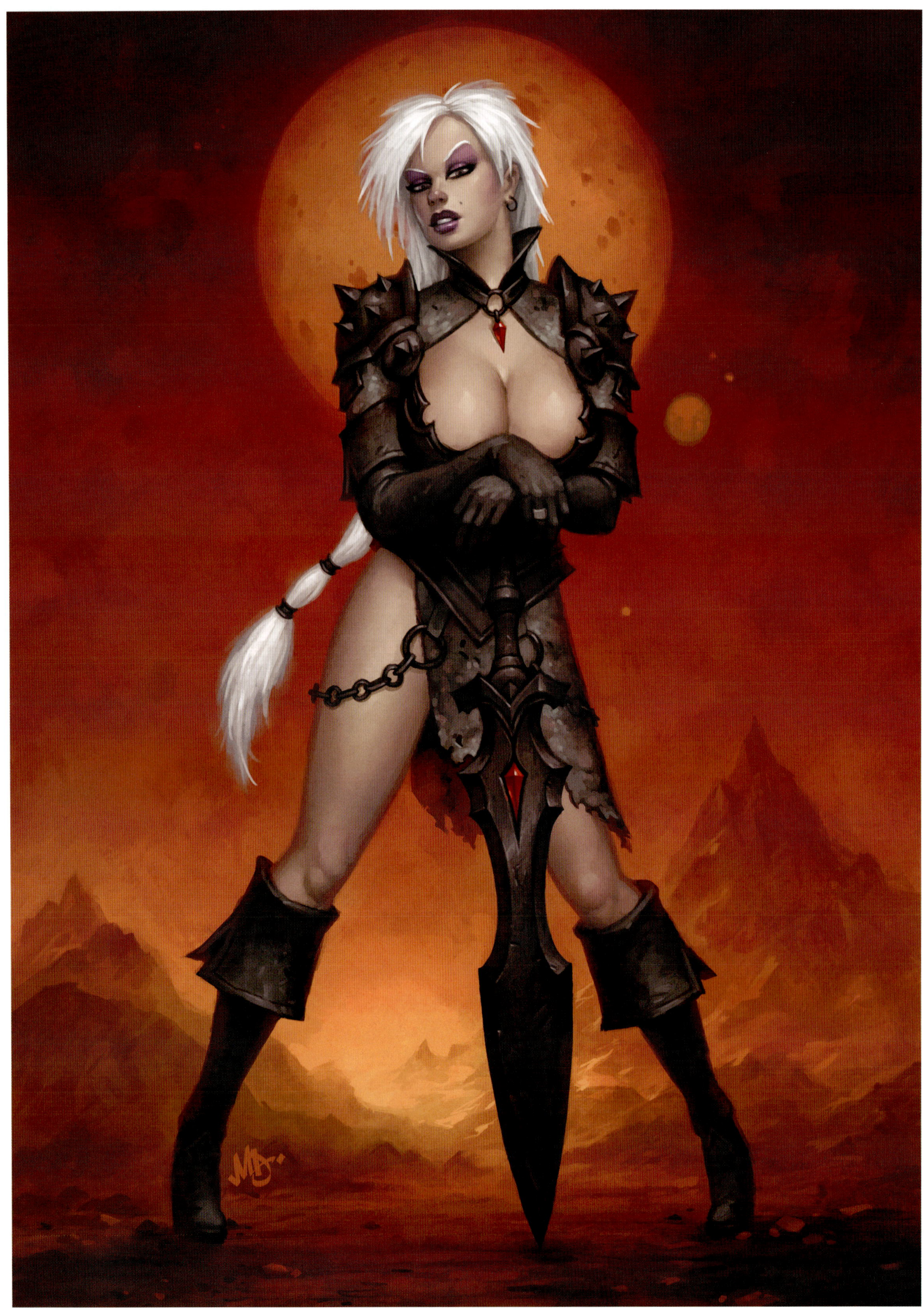

Black Sword

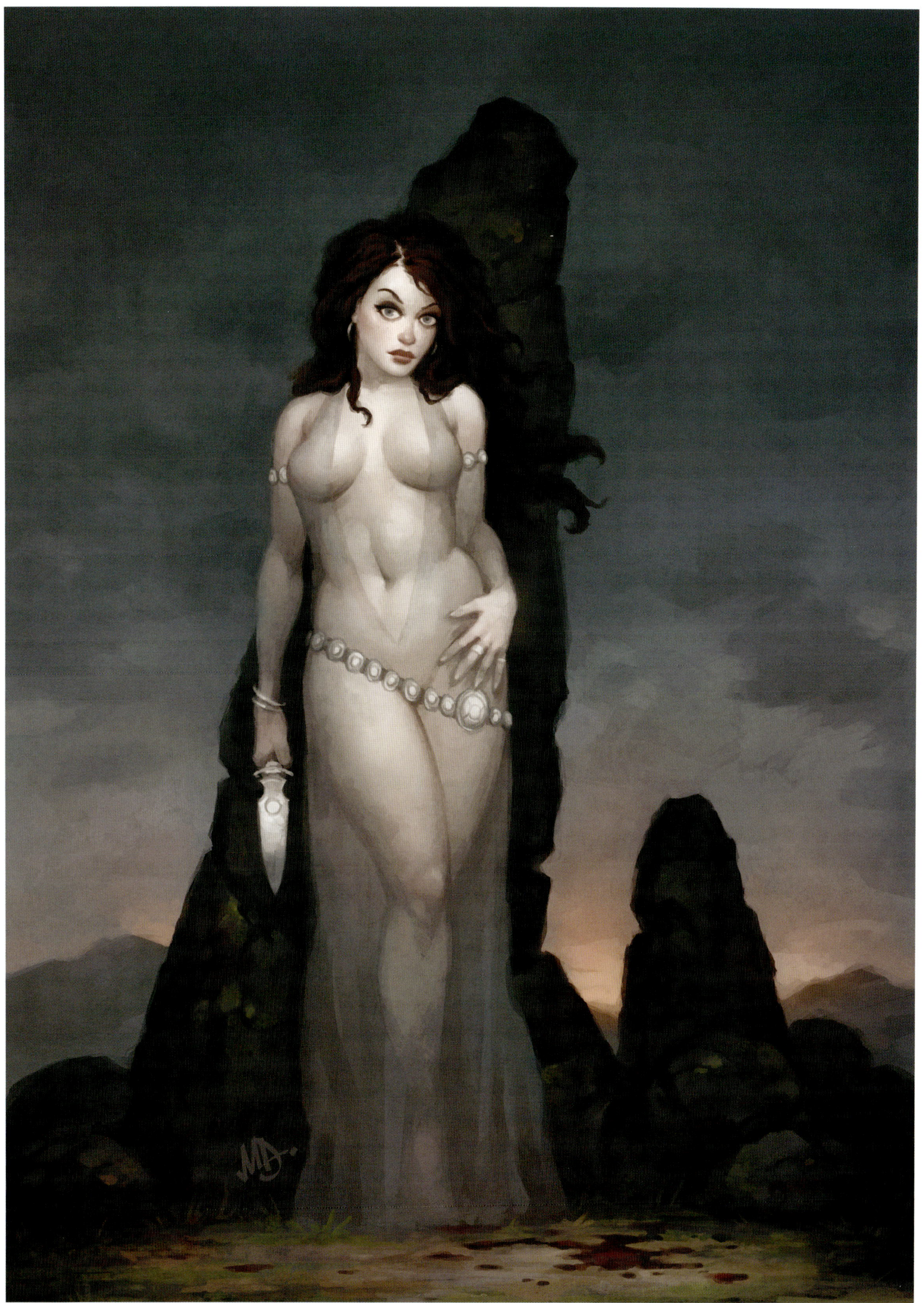

Ritual

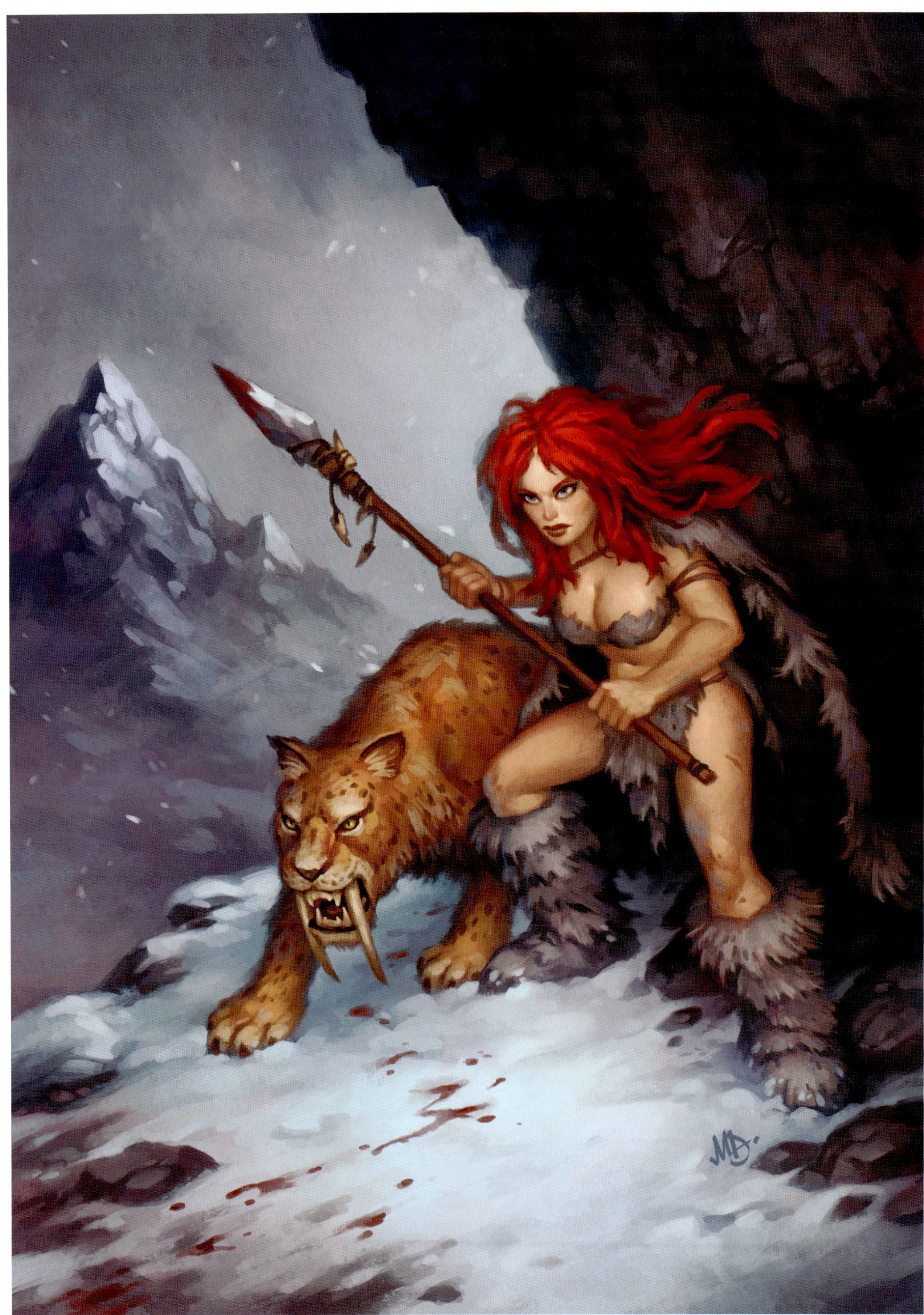

Snow Hunters

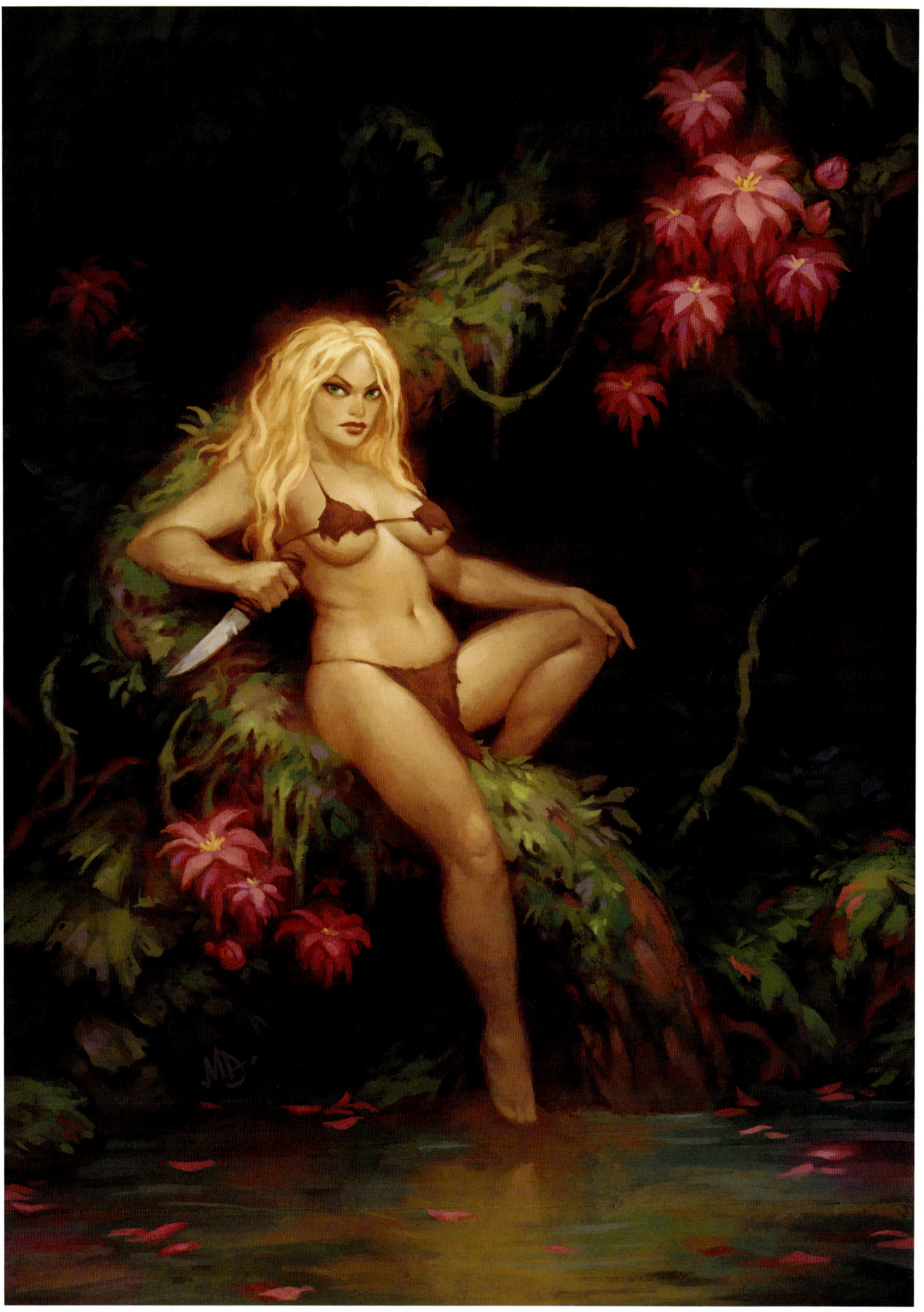

Jungle Guardian

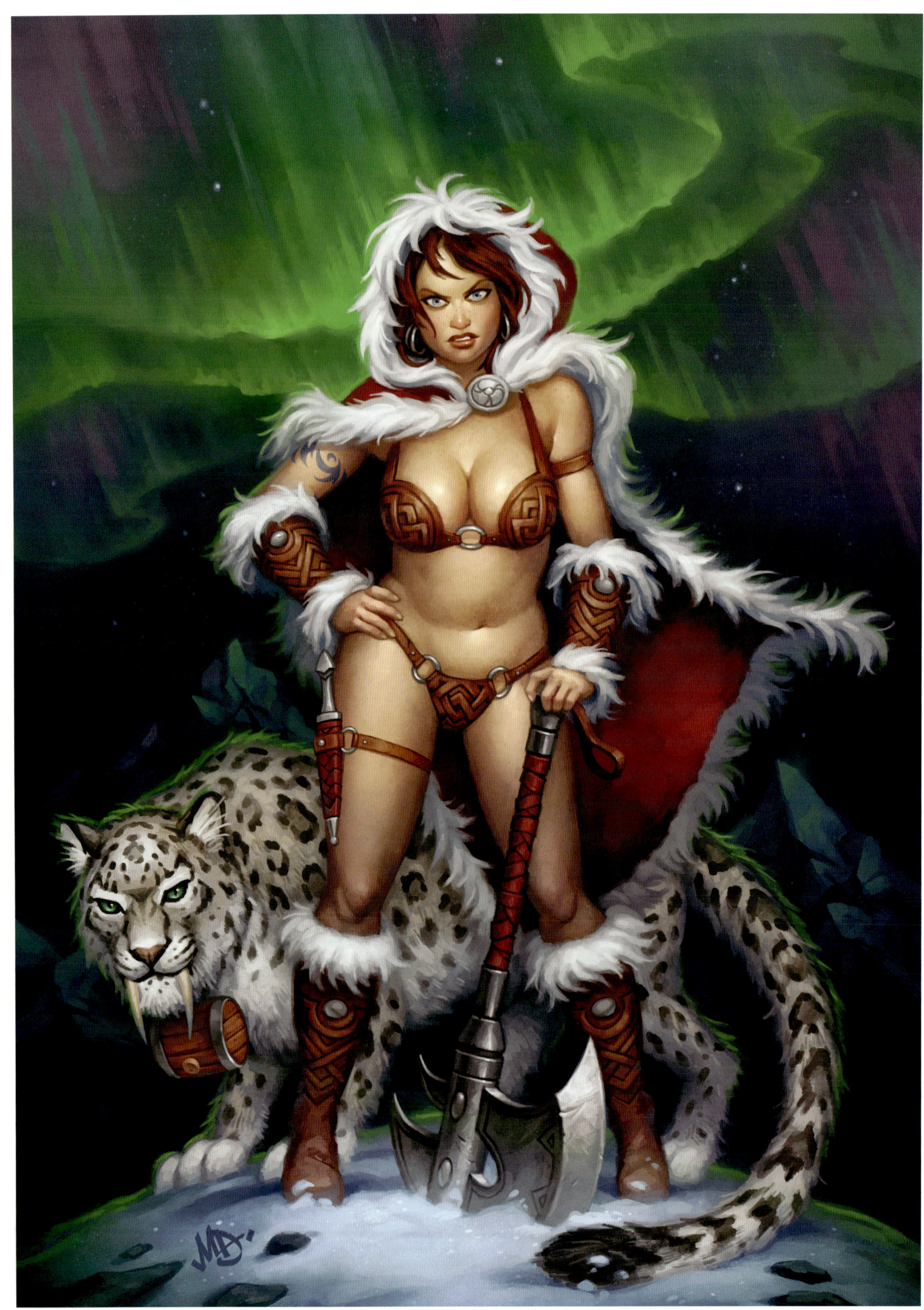

Aneira Coldthigh

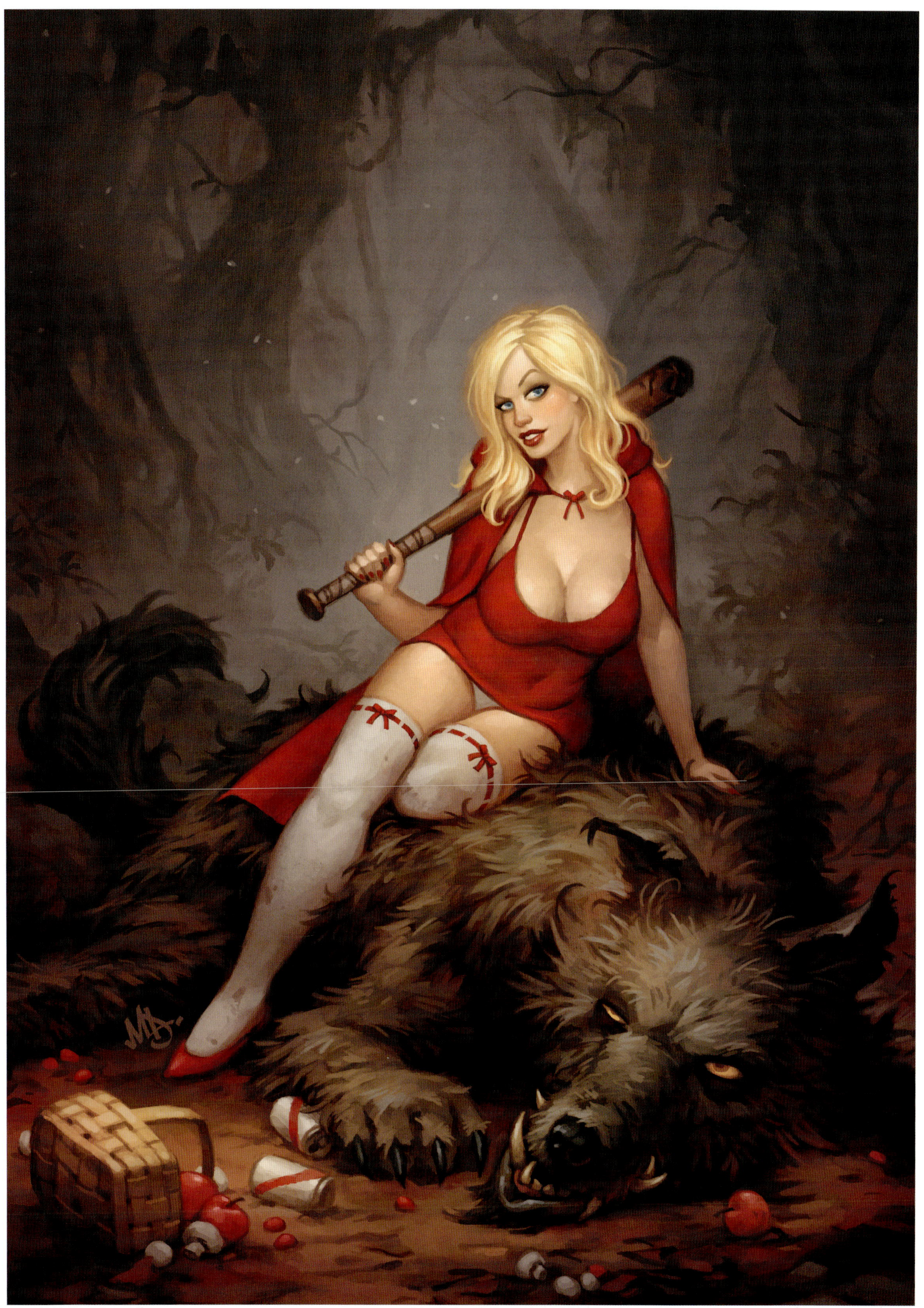

Red's Revenge

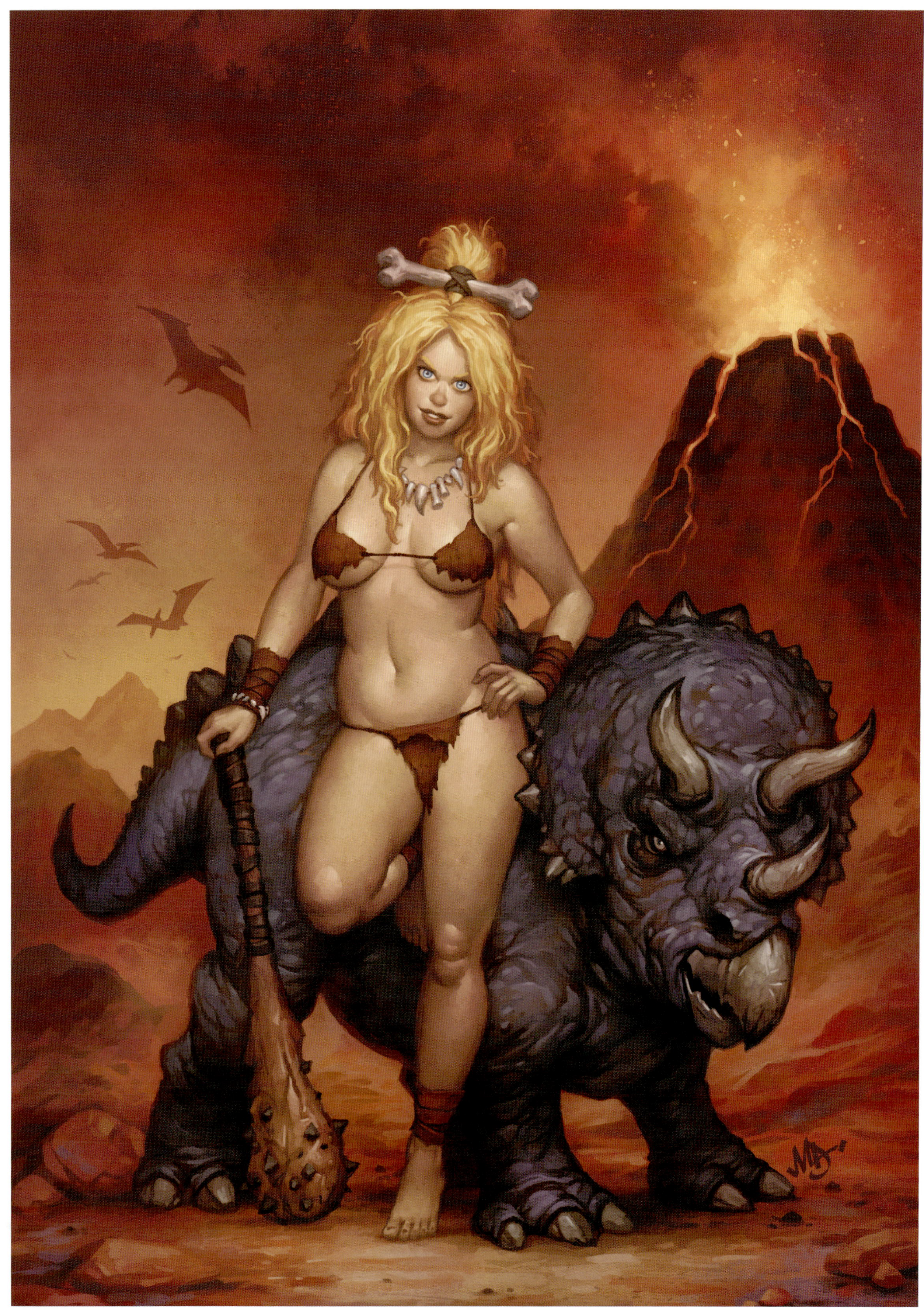

Let's Go Clubbing

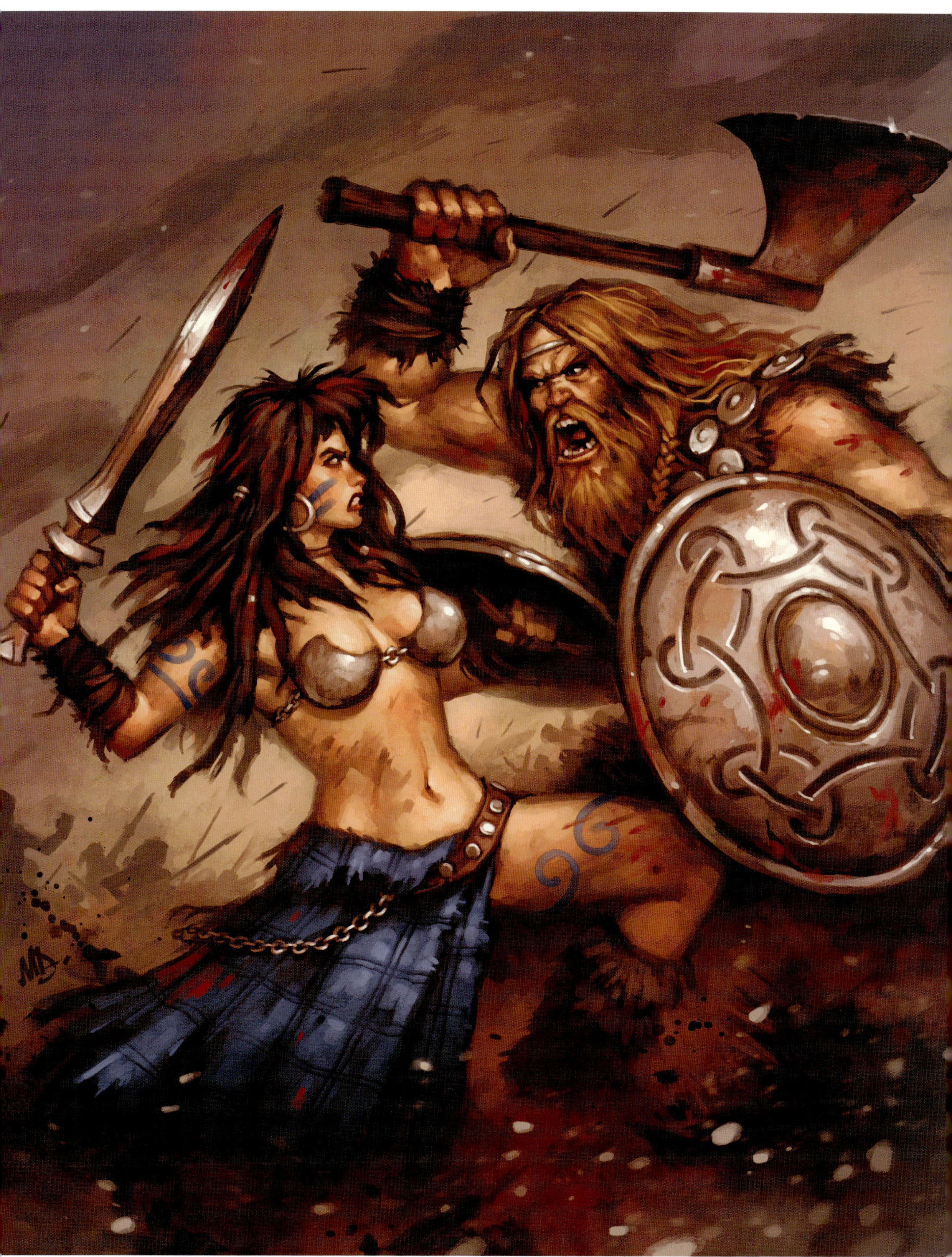

Battle Metal

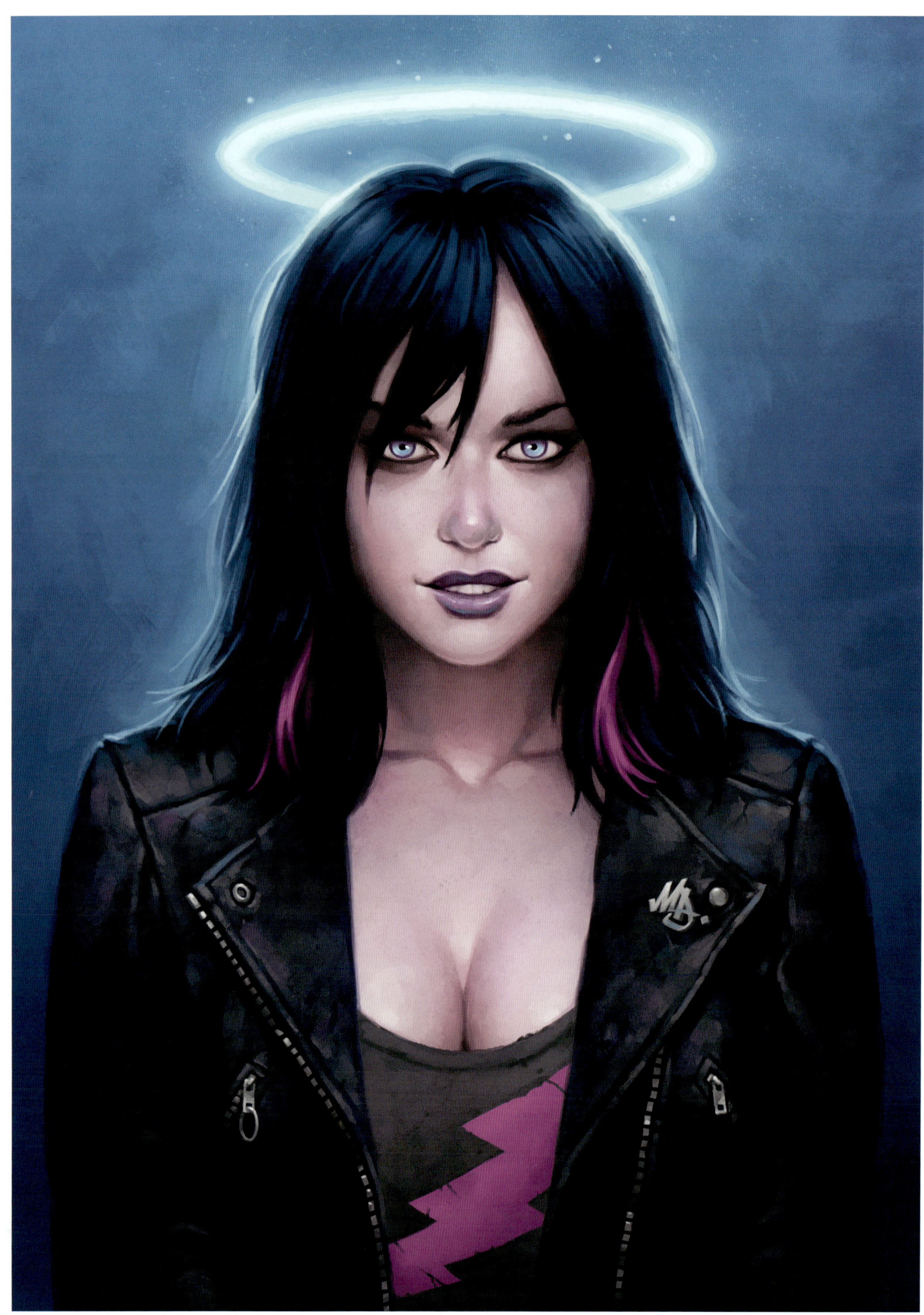

Electric Angel

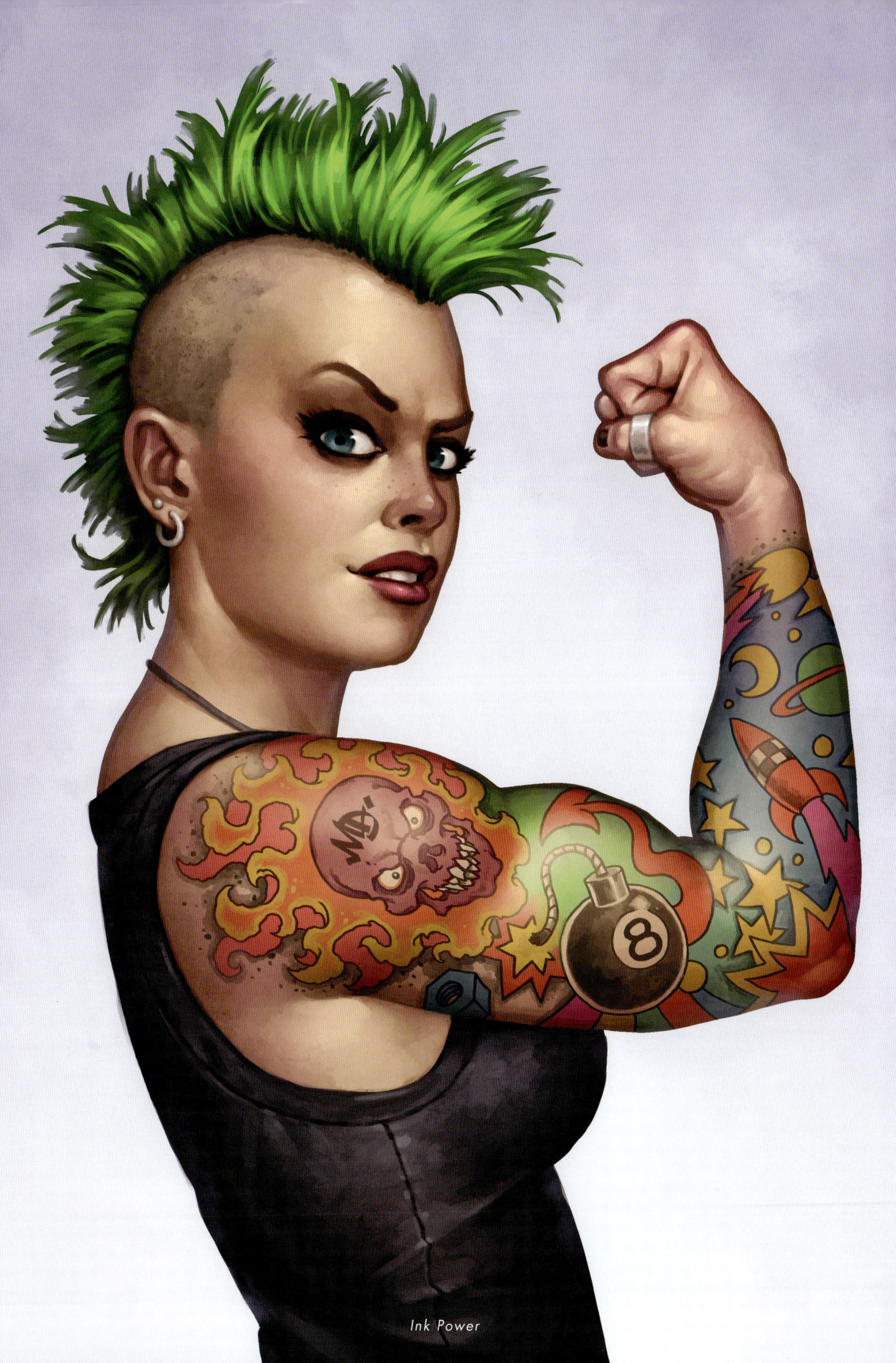

Ink Power

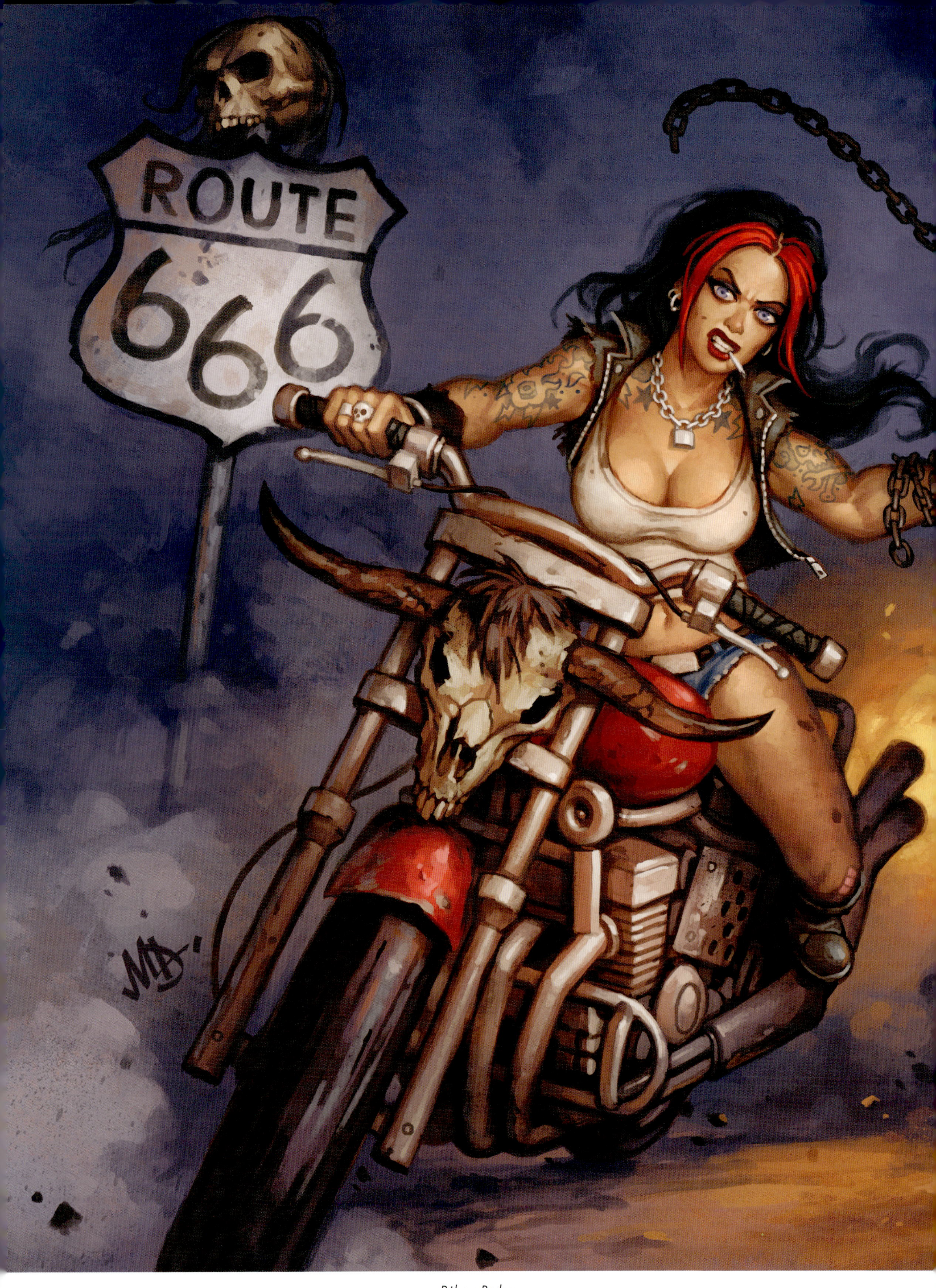

Biker Babe

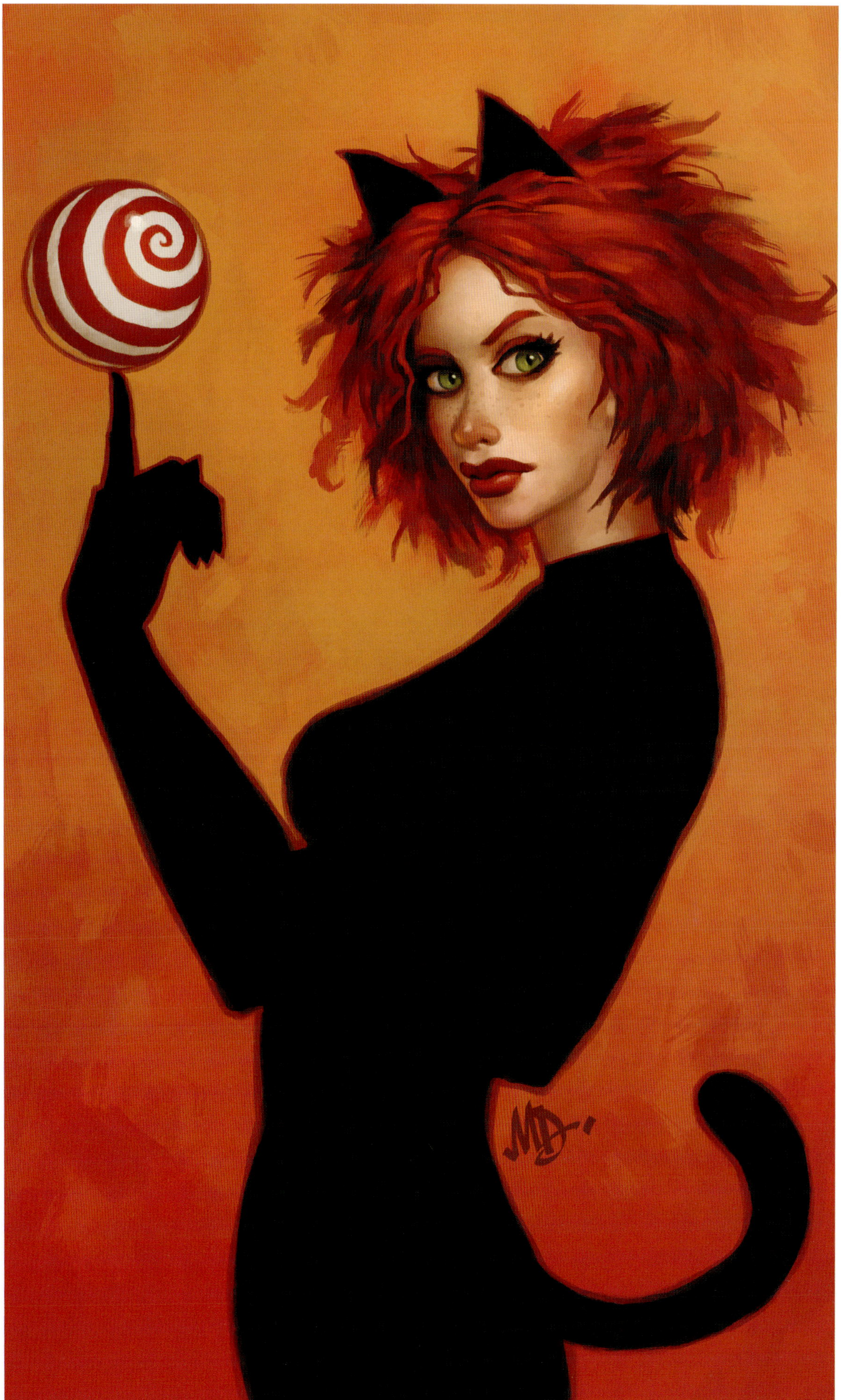

Meow

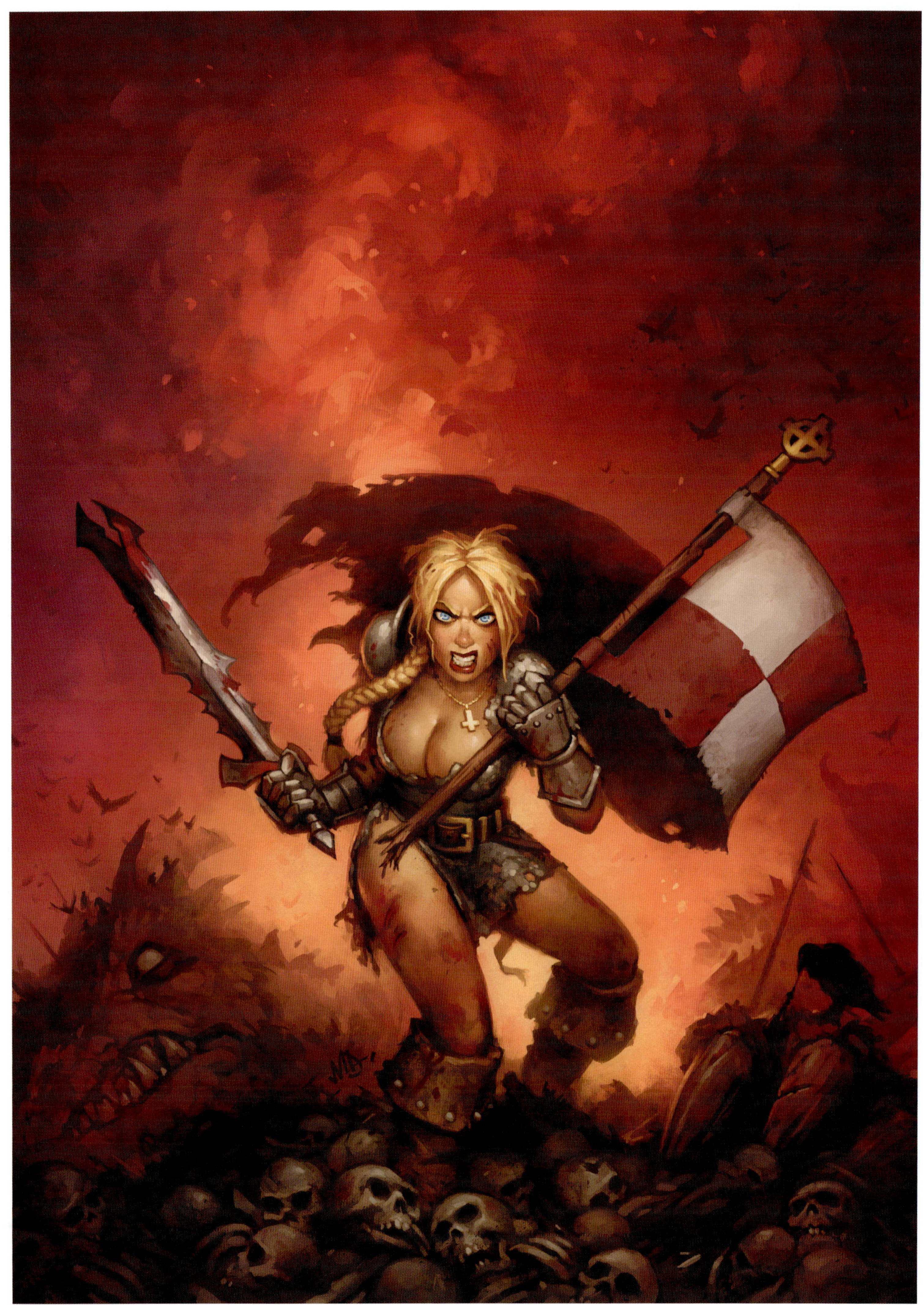

No Guts, No Glory

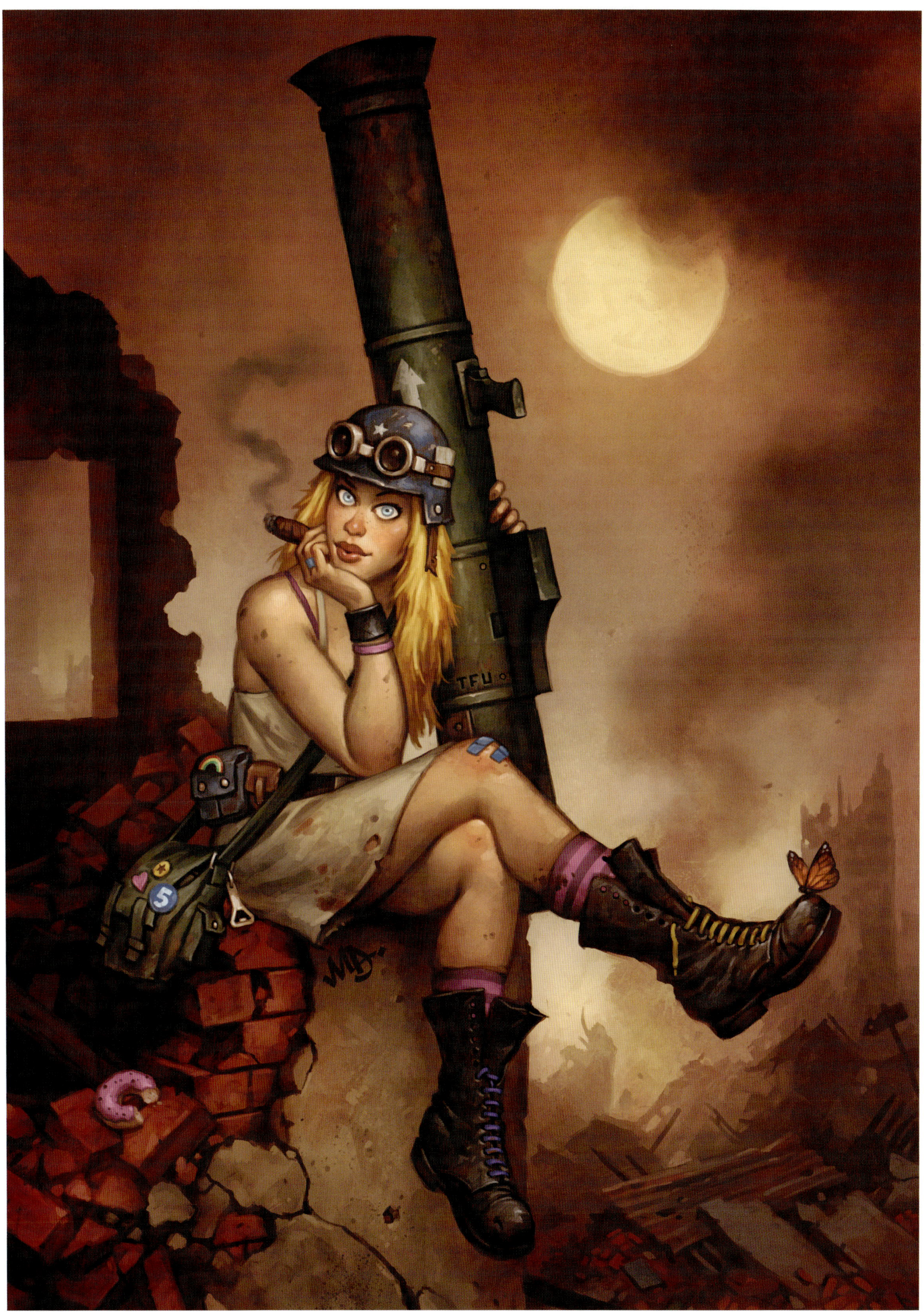

Bazooka Betty

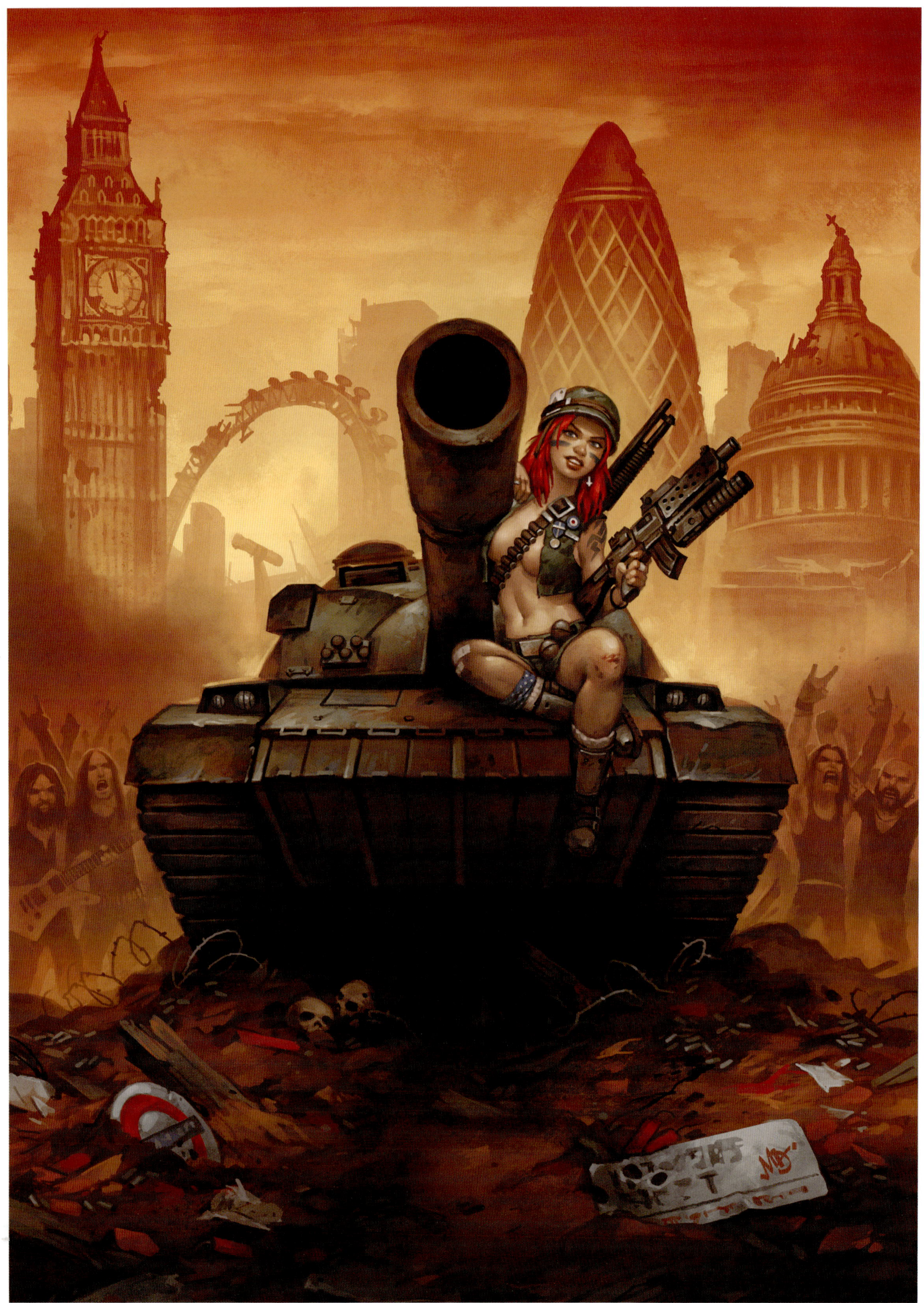

Golden Gods 2012

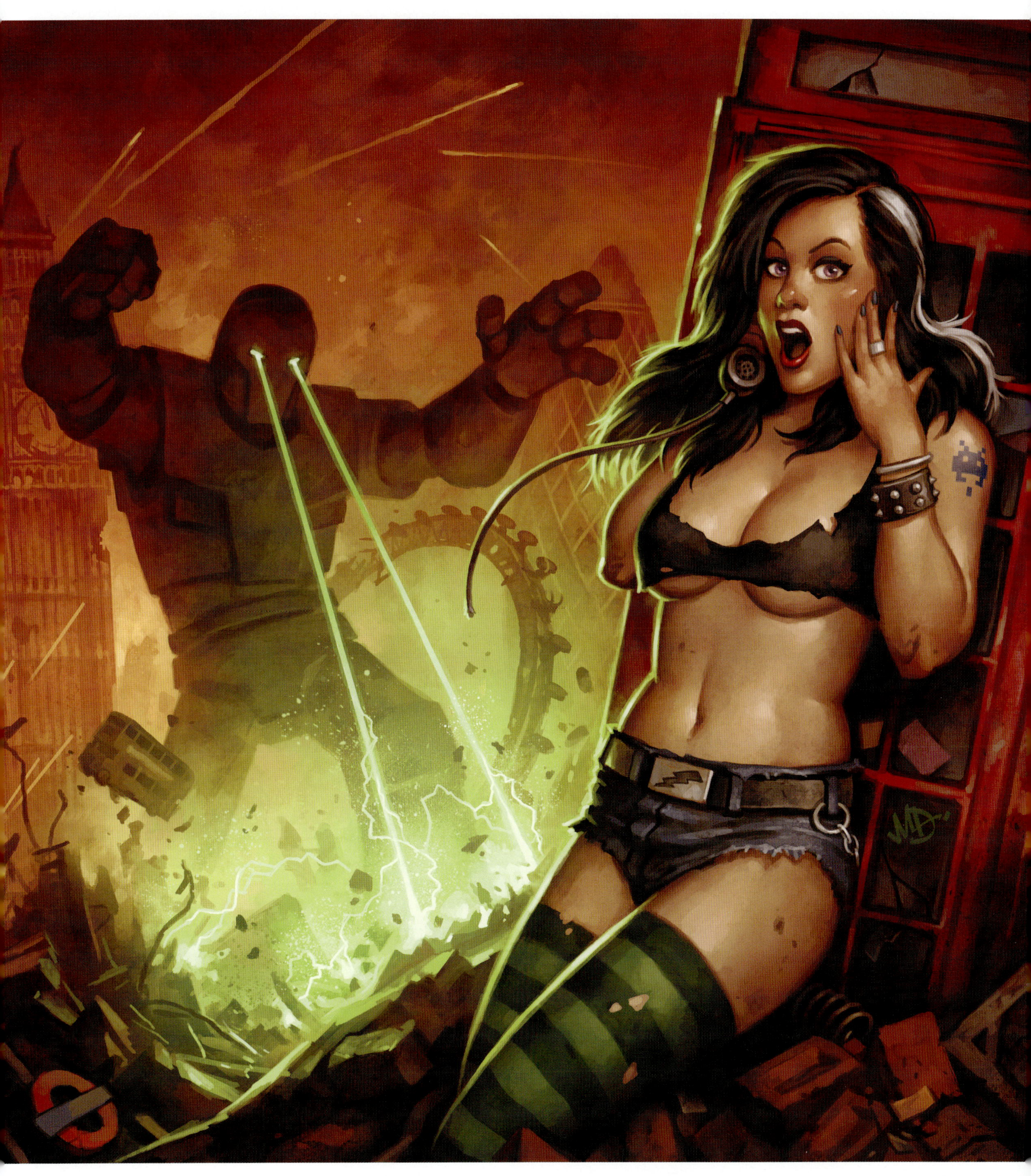

Attack of the Metal Gods

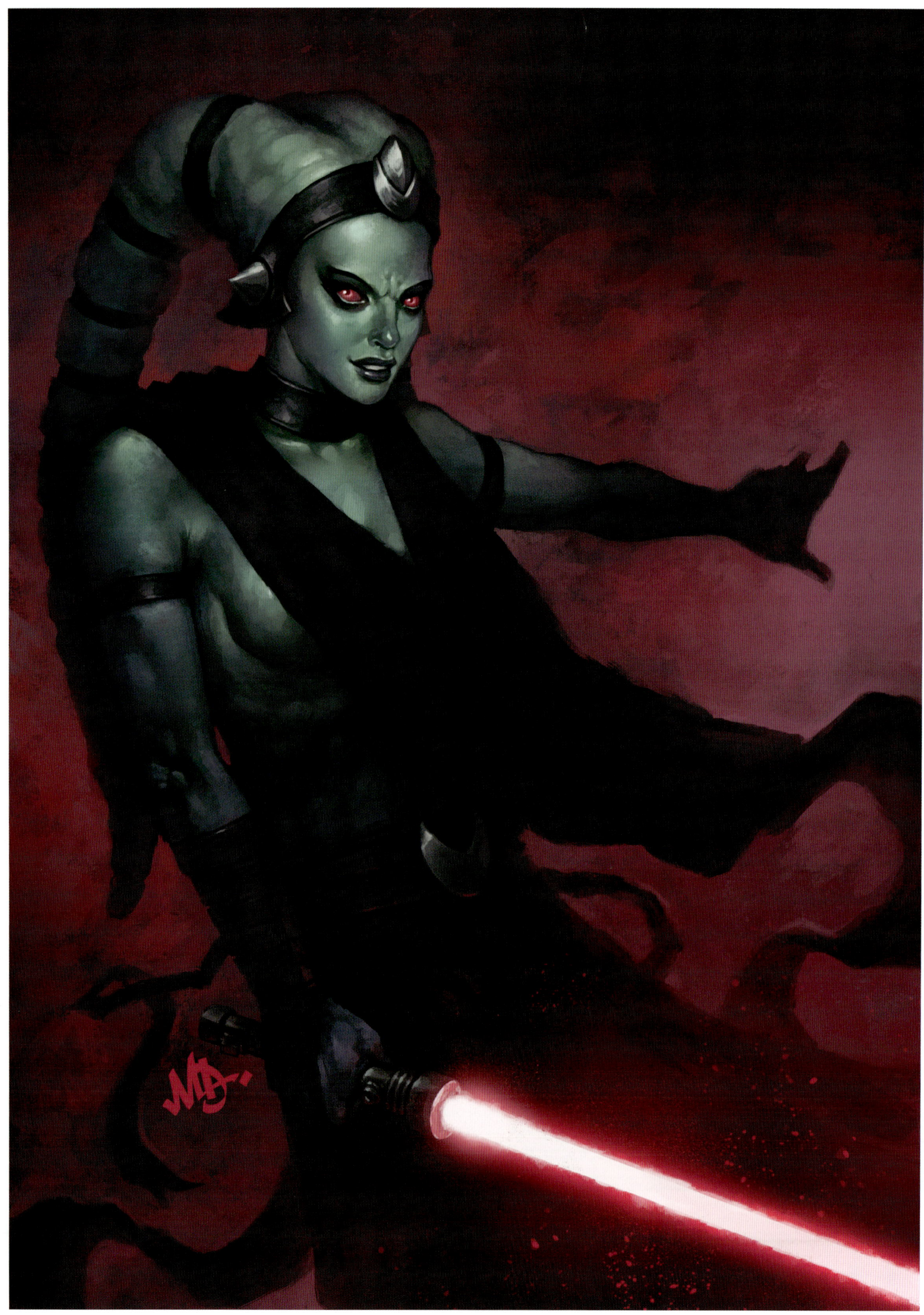

Darth Chuckles

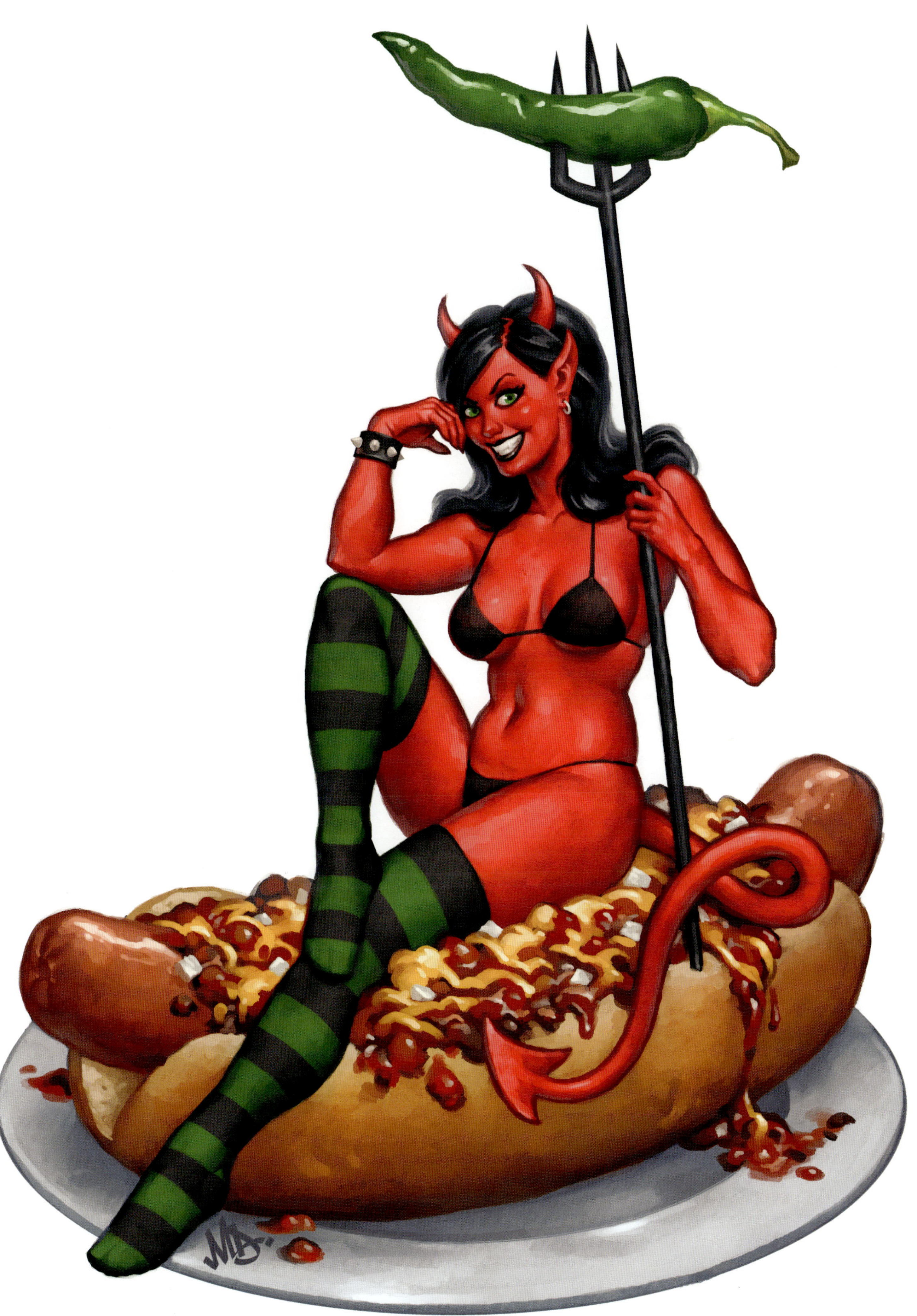

Elle Diablo

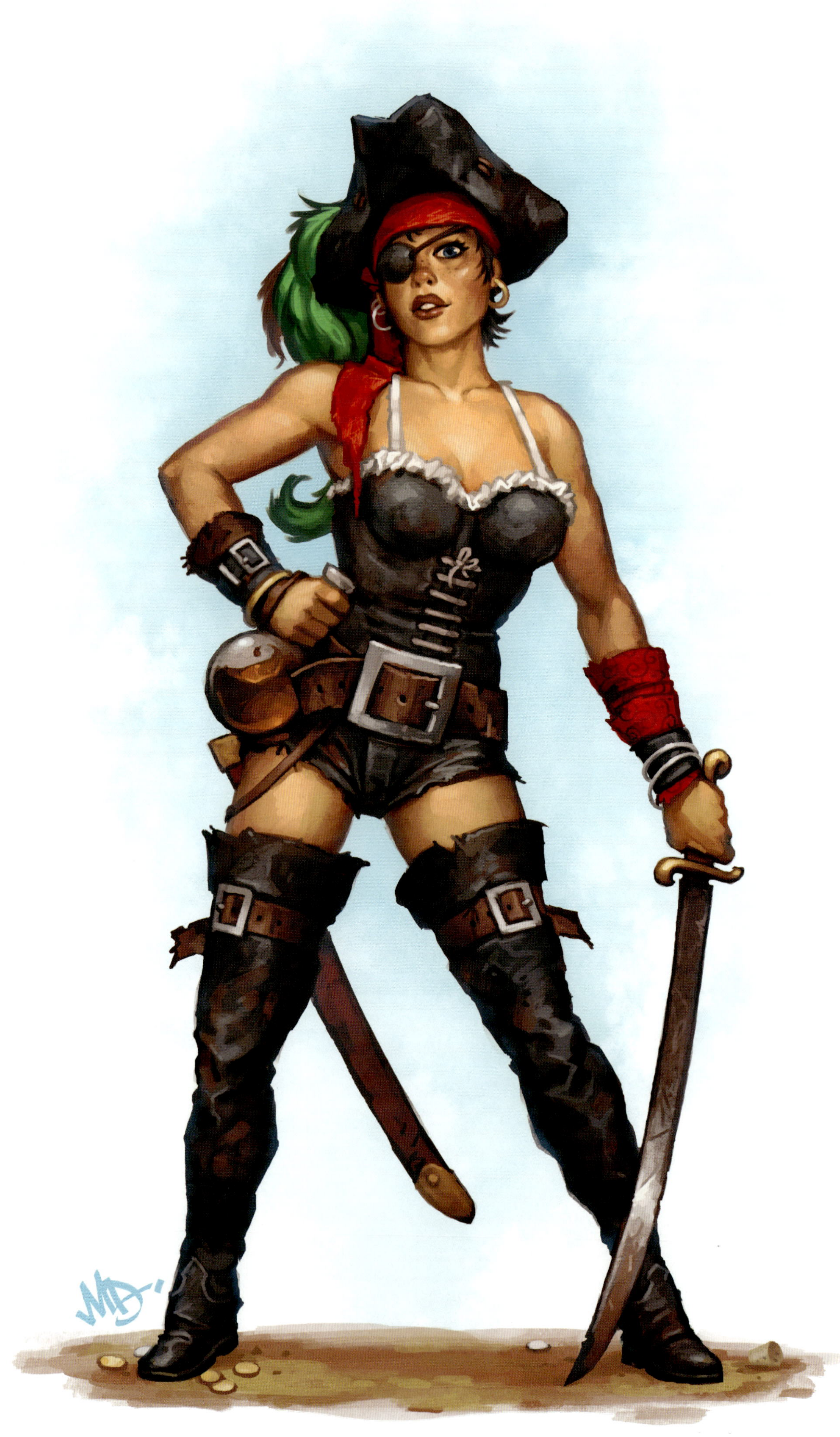

Swashbuckler

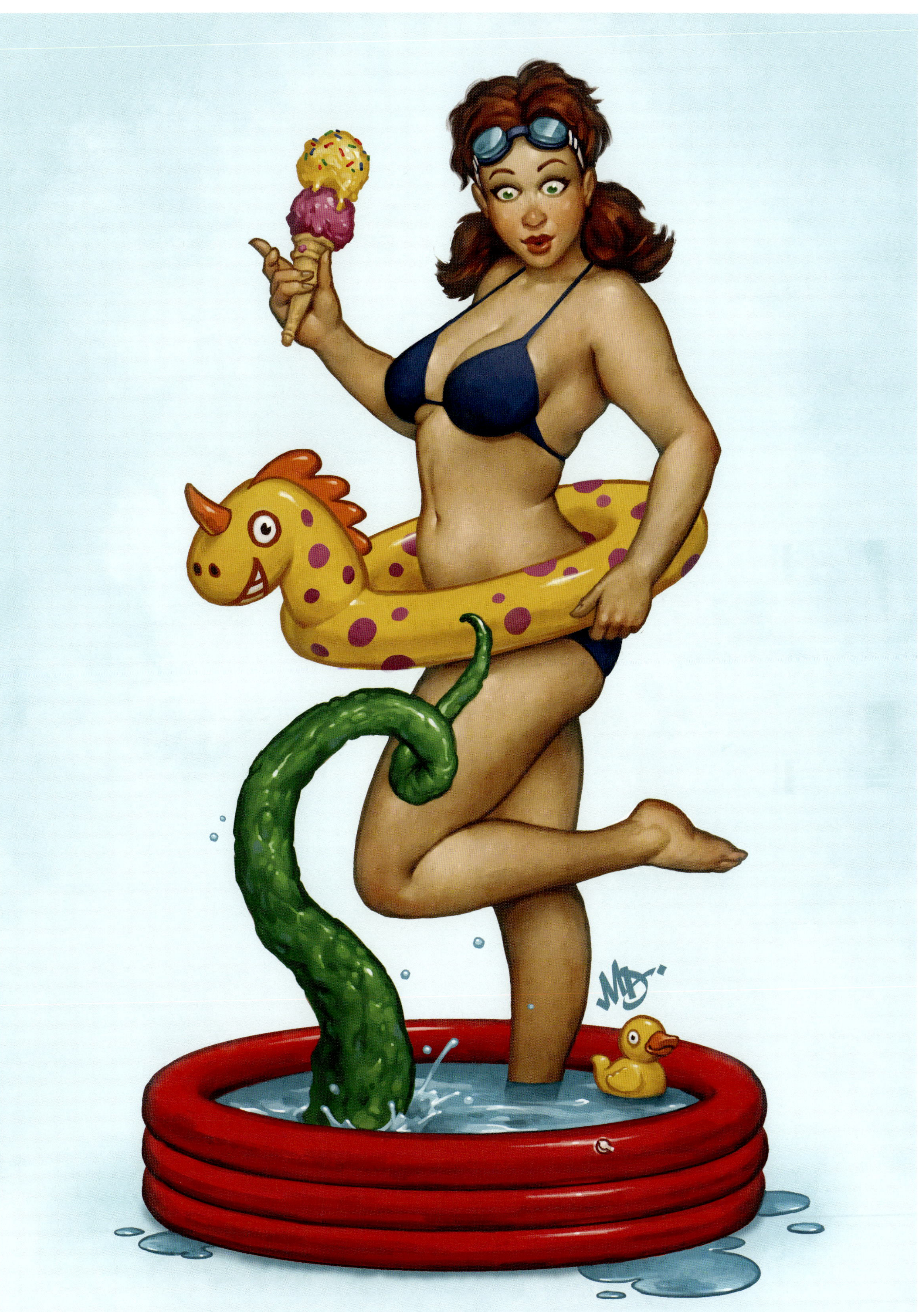

Pool Pals

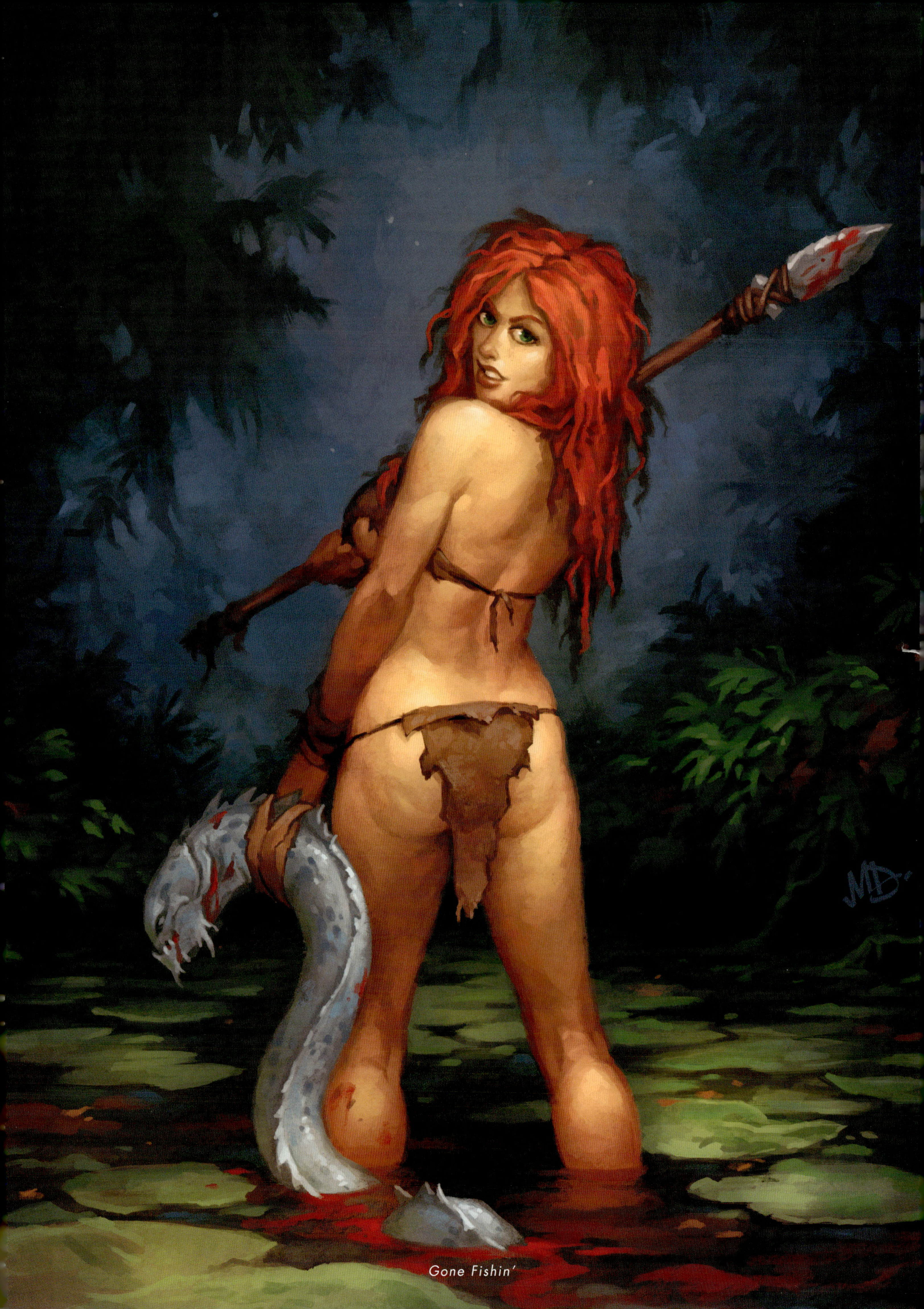

Gone Fishin'